basketball

ENLARGED EDITION including official rules of the game

ATHLETIC
INSTITUTE
SERIES

By
Dr. Forrest C. "Phog" Allen
Harold E. "Bud" Foster
Edward S. "Eddie" Hickey

 STERLING PUBLISHING CO., INC.   NEW YORK

 The Oak Tree Press   LONDON AND SYDNEY

ATHLETIC INSTITUTE SERIES

Revised Edition
Copyright © 1969, 1968, 1965 by
by The Athletic Institute
Published by Sterling Publishing Co., Inc.
419 Park Avenue South, New York 10016
British edition published in Great Britain and the Commonwealth by
The Oak Tree Press, Ltd., 116 Baker St., London, W.1.
Manufactured in the United States of America
Library of Congress Catalog Card No.: 65-20875
Standard Book Number 8069-4302 –5
UK 7061 2126 0   8069-4303 –3

Table of Contents

THE BASKETBALL COURT

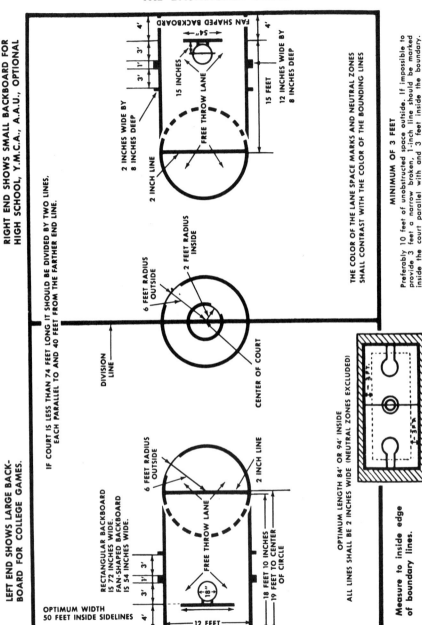

LEFT END SHOWS LARGE BACK-BOARD FOR COLLEGE GAMES.

RIGHT END SHOWS SMALL BACKBOARD FOR HIGH SCHOOL, Y.M.C.A., A.A.U., OPTIONAL

IF COURT IS LESS THAN 74 FEET LONG IT SHOULD BE DIVIDED BY TWO LINES, EACH PARALLEL TO AND 40 FEET FROM THE FARTHER END LINE.

FAN SHAPED BACKBOARD

←54"→

15 INCHES

2 INCHES WIDE BY 8 INCHES DEEP

2 INCH LINE

FREE THROW LANE

15 FEET

12 INCHES WIDE BY 8 INCHES DEEP

4'   3' 1' 3'

DIVISION LINE

CENTER OF COURT

2 FEET RADIUS INSIDE

6 FEET RADIUS OUTSIDE

RECTANGULAR BACKBOARD IS 72 INCHES WIDE. FAN-SHAPED BACKBOARD IS 54 INCHES WIDE.

6 FEET RADIUS OUTSIDE

2 INCH LINE

FREE THROW LANE

18"

18 FEET 10 INCHES 19 FEET TO CENTER OF CIRCLE

OPTIMUM WIDTH 50 FEET INSIDE SIDELINES

4'   3' 1' 3'

12 FEET

OPTIMUM LENGTH 84' OR 94' INSIDE ALL LINES SHALL BE 2 INCHES WIDE (NEUTRAL ZONES EXCLUDED)

THE COLOR OF THE LANE SPACE MARKS AND NEUTRAL ZONES SHALL CONTRAST WITH THE COLOR OF THE BOUNDING LINES.

MINIMUM OF 3 FEET

Preferably 10 feet of unobstructed space outside. If impossible to provide 3 feet a narrow broken, 1-inch line should be marked inside the court parallel with and 3 feet inside the boundary.

3'

3'

Measure to inside edge of boundary lines.

1. The Game

Basketball is one of the few major sports that originated entirely in the United States. Other games, as we know them today, evolved from sports of other lands. But basketball is as American as the national anthem. It started in 1891 when Dr. James Naismith used a peach basket and a soccer ball to invent a new game for athletes to play during the period between football and baseball seasons.

He suspended the peach basket above the gymnasium floor and made a game of trying to throw the ball into the basket. So sound was his idea that from this simple beginning there developed the modern game of basketball—easy to understand, easy to play, yet so healthful and stimulating that it has more participants than any other team sport, and so thrilling to watch that it can boast greater total attendance than any other sport in the country.

The Y.M.C.A. carried the game around the world. In every civilized country, its popularity grew until now it is played in

every corner of the globe, and its rules have been translated into more than thirty different languages.

Modern basketball is fast, requiring sudden bursts of speed and instant stops that frequently have its players traveling as fast as the fastest sprinters—so fast that in some situations the ball is passed at speeds up to 41 miles an hour.

And yet, even at such great speeds, the game of basketball demands the finest of control and coordination. It demands stamina. In a hard game, and at such speeds, players will often run as much as 4 or 5 miles during the course of the game. Above all, it demands the calm precision and accurate control

that enables a player to find his target quickly in the rush and pressure of the game and to shoot accurately over long distances.

A further requirement, and an essential one, is what basketball players call wide-angle vision—the ability to look straight ahead and still see and recognize players on both sides. You

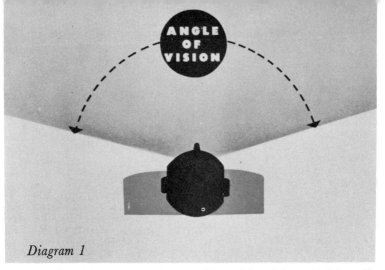

Diagram 1

must be able to see action on either side without looking, if you expect to play successful basketball (Diagram 1).

The regulation basketball court is a rectangle with certain maximum and minimum dimensions. The largest a court may be is 94 feet long by 50 feet wide, which is used by players of college age and older. A court 84 feet by 50 feet is used for high school players, and the smallest court, 74 feet long by 42 feet wide is permissible for players of early high school age or younger (Diagram 2).

Diagram 2

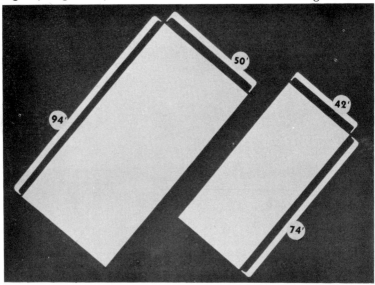

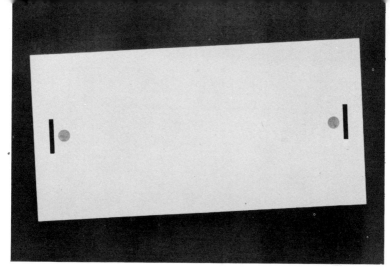

Diagram 3

In the middle of each end of the playing area are the basket and backboards. The backboards are inside the court, 4 feet from the back boundary line (Diagram 3). Under each basket is a free-throw lane stretching out toward the center of the court and ending in a free-throw circle. The lane is 12 feet wide. The center of the circle is 15 feet from the backboard and the outer edge of the circle is 25 feet from the boundary line (Diagram 4).

Diagram 4

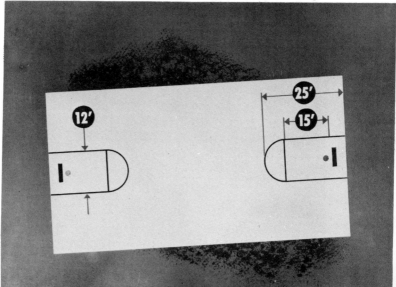

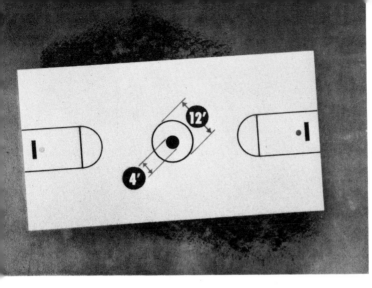

Diagram 5

In the exact middle of the court is a circle 4 feet in diameter, called the center circle. Outside the center circle is another circle 12 feet in diameter, called the restraining circle. This is the same size as the free-throw circles and all three circles serve the same purpose—to keep players back the correct distance on jump balls inside the circles (Diagram 5). A line across the middle divides the court into two equal parts, called the back court and the front court (Diagram 6).

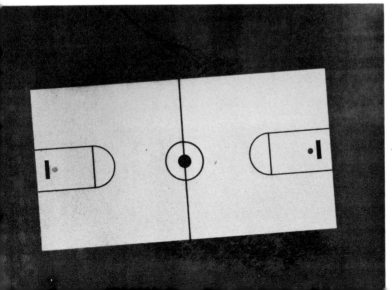

Diagram 6

The board behind the basket is made of wood, glass, plastic, or metal, and is called the backboard. There are two basic types—a square type, 6 feet wide and 4 feet high, and a fan-shaped backboard. The fan-shaped board is regulation for high school basketball, although the square board is permissible where the gym is already equipped with that type. Transparent backboards are also official for collegiate basketball.

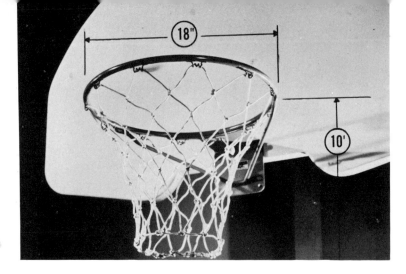

The baskets are white cord nets, open at both ends, suspended from a metal ring 18 inches in diameter and hung on the backboard 10 feet from the floor.

The ball weighs between 20 and 22 ounces, and holds from 7 to 9 pounds of air. It may not be less than 29 inches in circumference and not more than 30.

Personal equipment for basketball is simply shirt, trunks, and sturdy, rubber-soled shoes. Opposing teams usually wear contrasting colors for quick and easy identification during play. Five men form a basketball team—a center, two forwards and two guards. (Diagram 7 shows their starting positions.)

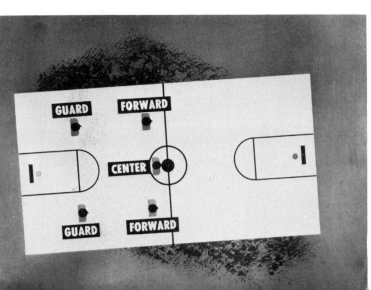

Diagram 7

14

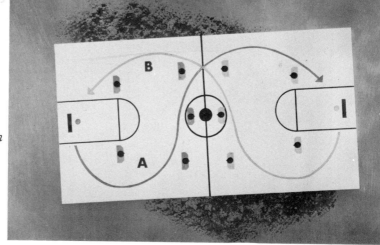

Diagram 8

When a game starts, Team A and B each try to score baskets at opposite ends of the floor. The defending team tries to prevent the team in possession of the ball from reaching its basket (Diagram 8).

The game is divided into certain time periods. The high school game is made up of four 8-minute periods with a 2-minute intermission between quarters and a 10-minute intermission between halves. The college game consists of two 20-minute periods with a 15-minute intermission between halves.

The referee puts the ball in play with a center jump: The referee tosses the ball between the two opposing centers, and each tries to jump up and tap the ball toward a team mate.

15

When a player gets the ball he tries to advance it toward his own basket—the one the opposing team is guarding. He must not run with the ball—but must dribble it. It's a violation of the rules to take more than one step while either hand is touching the ball.

He must advance the ball while it is in his possession by dribbling—which is running and bouncing the ball as he goes. In this way his hand is not in contact with the ball for more

than a single step at a time. However, if he stops his dribble and touches the ball with both hands, he cannot dribble again. He must get rid of the ball either by passing it to a teammate or shooting at the basket.

There are no restrictions on how he may pass. He can pass overhand or underhand, with one hand or two hands. He can throw it through the air, bounce it or roll it across the floor, or

he can hand it to a teammate. There are no restrictions on shooting either. Here, too, he may shoot overhand or underhand, with one hand or two.

A team scores by tossing the ball through its own basket from the top downward. The ball must enter from the top and come out through the bottom. After a score the ball becomes

dead. To put it back in play, the team that did not score takes it out of bounds under the basket and throws or bounces it into the playing area. Then play resumes just as before.

For certain infractions of the rules, the penalty is one or two free throws awarded to the team which was fouled. One player (the player fouled in most instances) stands behind the line in the free-throw circle and tries to throw the ball through his

1 POINT

basket. If he succeeds in getting the ball through the basket on a free throw, his team scores one point for each successful throw.

On every basket made during play, the team making the basket receives two points. This is known as a field goal. The team that scores the most points from both types of baskets wins.

2 POINTS

There are many other rules in basketball, which are all given in the official rules at the back of this book. Every beginning basketball player should study the rules until he knows all thoroughly.

Basketball can be one of the fastest, most dazzling of all team sports. It requires excellent team work with perfect coordination between players. But most important, before perfect cooperation is possible, every player must be competent in all phases of the game—in ball handling, dribbling, passing, shooting, guarding and maneuvering. And he must learn to do all this with a minimum of bodily contact with his opponent. Not roughness but skill, not brute strength but endurance and stamina, are the keys to success in basketball.

2. Ball Handling

There are few sports in which there is such unrelenting competition as in basketball. There are no let-downs, no coasting periods. During every minute of the game every player's attention has to be concentrated on gaining possession of the ball.

Since all activity in every game is centered around the ball itself, the first fundamental of winning basketball is skill in ball handling. By ball handling is meant the position of your hands on the ball and the action of your hands when holding the ball, whether you are preparing to dribble, pass or shoot. It starts, of course, with receiving.

In a game you will have to receive the ball in any number of strained and difficult positions. You have to take it wherever it comes to you. In these cases, no matter what the position of your hands and body, your first move on gaining possession of the ball should be to get your body under control and the ball properly positioned for play.

Photo 1

Let's begin ball handling with the correct position of hands on the ball. The most effective position is shown in Photo 1—the fingers and thumbs spread evenly around the sides of the ball, the heels of the hands to the rear and both hands a little behind the center of the ball.

One of the most important rules of ball handling is: *Never hold the ball in the palms of your hands.* Notice in Photo 2 how the ball rests on the cushiony part of the fingers and thumbs, not on the palms. The palms of your hands should never touch the ball except for a very brief moment when you receive it.

Photo 2

24

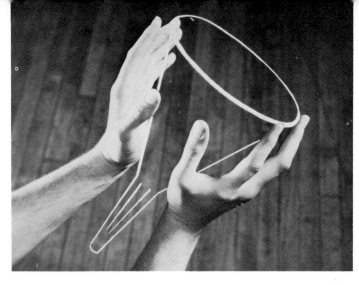

Photo 3

Now, if you take the ball out of those hands and leave them in exactly the same position, you'll notice they are positioned like the sides of a funnel (Photo 3). The purpose of this position is to form a backstop for the ball when it comes to you so that hard throws won't go through. Your fingers act as a cushion and brake on the ball, and serve to trap it when it reaches you.

To assume that position, first place your hands in the funnel shape, the heels of your wrists forming the neck of the funnel (Step 1).

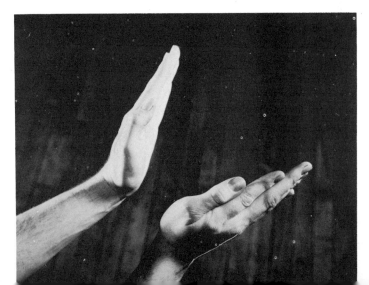

Step 1

25

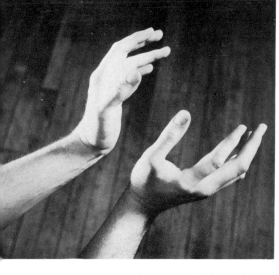

Then relax your hands as shown in Step 2, with your fingers and thumbs spread wide apart and your fingertips flexed inward so they will contact the ball first when it is passed to you. With your hands in that position, pick up a ball (Step 3). It should rest easily on the cushions of your fingers and thumbs—not on your palms at all. And you should have a feeling of firm control. Practice holding the ball this way, moving it around in front of you, until you can feel that control without using the palms of your hands.

Now let's see the proper action for receiving. Photo 1 shows your hand position from in front. Now imagine a ball is being passed to you from directly in front. That is the most basic pass in the game. By learning it, you can learn all the fundamentals of receiving. To receive it you should move your body toward it.

Step 3   *Photo 1*

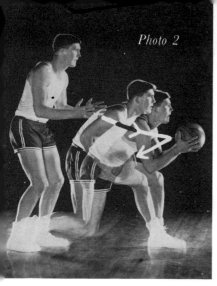

Photo 2

Step 1

Photo 2 shows the complete movement—it's a swooping movement forward to meet the ball and then back with the ball as it reaches your hands. Let's try the forward swoop first.

Bend forward slightly at the waist to get set, with your hands about waist high in front of you (Step 1). Then stride toward the ball, bending your knees and waist in the swooping movement, reaching forward for the ball. Keep your hips low (Step 2).

Step 2

Step 3

Now without stopping, begin the recoil movement after the ball reaches your hands—push back with your forward foot and bring your hands back toward your body (Step 3).

That's all there is to the fundamental movement of receiving. Swoop forward to meet the ball and recoil back with it. Practice this complete movement, shown in Step 4, until it flows easily without any jerking or stabbing. Don't grab at the ball, just move forward to meet it and come back with it.

Step 4

Step 1

Now let's try it with the ball. As the ball comes toward you, you'll sense the moment to start the forward swooping movement (Step 1). Continue in stride and time your movement so that when the ball is just out of reach your arms are fully extended forward (Step 2).

Step 2

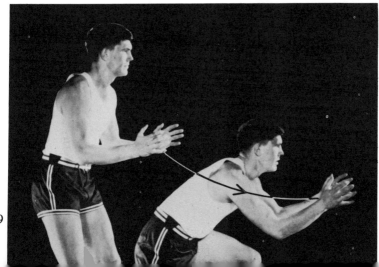

That's the moment, just before the ball reaches your hand, that you start your recoil movement. Start back before the ball reaches you and let it catch up with you (Step 3). Now all your movement is backward, with the ball. Cushion the ball in your fingers during that backward movement (Step 4).

Step 4

The complete movement begins with striding forward and reaching toward the ball. Start back just before it reaches your hands, and catch it on the way back. Don't stab or grab. It's an easy flowing movement that will become natural to you with practice. Remember that while this series of movements is used only for receiving a pass from straight in front, the fundamentals are similar in receiving all passes.

In actual play passes won't always come to you from directly in front. However, no matter what direction they come from and no matter what position you have to get into to receive them, the same fundamentals apply. Reach toward the ball as it comes to you, start back just before it reaches you and continue back in a recoil movement after it comes into your hands.

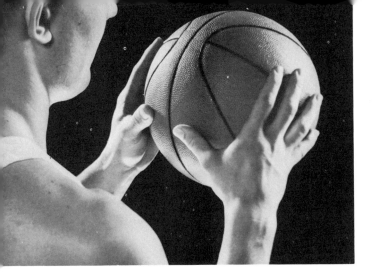

And always, as quickly as possible get back to the correct ball handling position. You have to be ready to pass, dribble or shoot and, if you always start from this position, you won't signal your next play to your opponents.

Since basketball is a game of continuous action, most of your catches will be made while you are in motion. Here is where you have to consider the direction of your movement. When you receive a ball on the run, try to be facing it and moving toward it whenever possible. But it isn't always possible.

32

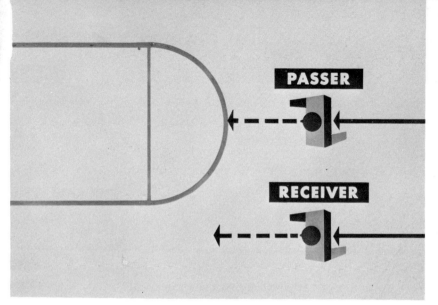

Diagram 1

For instance, when you're running parallel with the passer, you as the receiver can't move directly toward the ball (Diagram 1). Change your direction slightly—swing inward toward the ball to shorten the distance the ball has to travel, and thus lessen the chance that a nimble-footed opponent might steal it (Diagram 2). Your shoulders should be turned toward the ball as much as possible.

Diagram 2

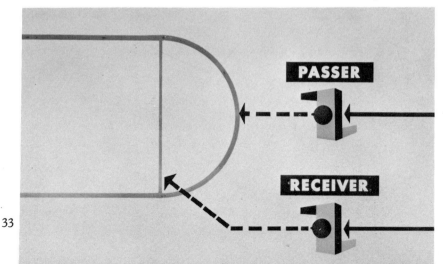

Ball handling is fundamental in basketball. Without this skill, basketball will be a difficult game for you, so study these basic movements and practice them until they are instinctive. When you have mastered them, you will be well on your way to winning basketball.

Photo 1

3. Passing

In basketball no one player can expect, nor should he try, to score by his own efforts alone. Most of the play consists of passing the ball between players and gradually working it down the floor and into scoring position. When a player with the ball finds his progress obstructed by an opposing player, he passes to a teammate in the clear, who in turn passes when his progress is stopped (Photos 1 and 2).

Photo 2

It's this constant exchanging of the ball that makes basketball the fast game it is. Thus skill at passing is important to every player. There are many types of passes. Let's study the fundamentals of some of the passes most used.

CHEST OR
PUSH PASS

The chest or push pass is probably used more than any other type of pass in the game. In the chest pass simply push the ball forward from your upper chest with a thrusting movement of your arms and body.

Step 1 shows the starting position—ball about chest high, hands a little behind the center of the ball and your fingers spread around the ball's surface. The first movement is down-

Step 1

Step 2

ward. To start the pass smoothly, drop your hands in a small circle away from you, and back up toward the original position (Step 2). But don't stop here. Keep the movement flowing smoothly as you change direction (Step 3). Just push the ball forward, straight toward the receiver. Don't snap it or throw it. Just push. And try to prevent the ball from spinning as it

Step 3

leaves your hands (Step 4). The faster the pass the less chance of its being intercepted.

Step 5 shows the complete arm movement. Practice it until it feels smooth and you have control. Then try it coordinated with the proper foot movement.

Step 5

Step 1

Step 2

In the starting position, your feet are parallel (Step 1). As you start your preliminary downward swing, step forward with whichever foot is more natural. Now your weight should be evenly distributed on both feet (Step 2). As the preliminary swing continues, bend your knees slightly into a slight crouch, ready to put the strength of your legs into the pass as well as your arms (Step 3).

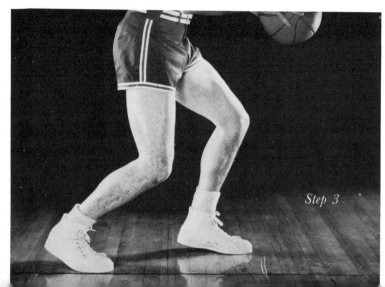

Step 3

Step 4

As you pass, straighten your knees, bringing your weight onto your forward foot as your body comes forward with the pass. As you complete the pass your weight is well forward and your arms are straight out in front of you in the direction of the pass (Step 4).

This over-the-shoulder pass is most effective for long or fast, hard passes. Essentially it consists of two basic movements—somewhat like a catcher's snap throw in baseball. First, use one hand to bring the ball back over your shoulder to a position behind your right ear. Then throw forward with a pushing movement, keeping your throwing hand behind the ball throughout the entire movement.

OVER-THE-SHOULDER PASS

Step 1   *Step 2*

Let's try the arm movement first. Step 1 gives your starting position—the fundamental ball handling position. From here you start by bringing the ball back into a cocked position behind your ear. Bring the ball back the shortest and fastest way—straight up and back. At the cocked position, just before your arm starts forward, your throwing forearm should be approximately perpendicular (Step 2). During this movement try to keep your other hand against the ball, balancing it until about the position shown in Step 3. Sometimes you may hold this position for an instant until your receiver is in the clear. Then start the ball forward.

Step 4 shows the full body movement as your body pivots

Step 3

Step 4

into the pass, and your throwing arm straightens forward. In the final push, just let the ball leave your hand with a full hand extension and follow through with your arm outstretched after the ball. Now let's see how this arm movement is coordinated with the movement of feet and body.

Step 1 gives your starting position, just as you receive the ball and bring it under control. Your weight is fairly evenly balanced on both feet. Now as you bring the ball back to the cocked position, your left shoulder turns toward the receiver. Step back with your right foot—quarter turn back to the right— and carry your weight back onto your right foot (Step 2). Now

Step 1

Step 2

43

Step 3

your weight is well back, ready to move forward with the pass.

As you start the ball forward, your weight goes forward too, adding the power of your legs and body to the pass (Step 3). At about this point in your pass your weight has shifted completely to your left foot, and as you continue forward you pivot slightly on your left foot, and your shoulders will come round with the pass. Let your right foot stride forward as you complete the pass (Step 4).

Step 4

44

Step 5

The complete forward movement of feet and body for the over-the-shoulder pass with one hand is shown in Step 5. Notice how the shoulders pivot behind the pass as your forward stride and body movement add power to your pass.

Study this pass and practice it from both the right and left sides, as a good passer must be able to pass from either side. It's a two-count rhythm—the first count is quick as the ball comes back, then a quick reversal, and the throw with feet, body, shoulders and arms.

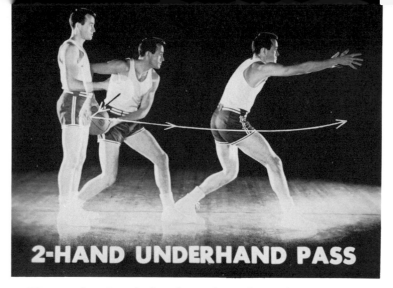

2-HAND UNDERHAND PASS

The two-hand underhand pass is used mostly after a stop or a pivot, but is often useful also for any short- or medium-length pass. It can be made either from the right or left side of the body, depending on the position of the receiver and your opponent.

These are the basic movements of the two-hand underhand pass. First the ball is drawn back to a position close to your hip, then passed—not thrown—forward with both hands. Both hands have an equal part in the pass and both hands leave the ball together.

Step 1

Step 2

As you start the pass, ball and feet move simultaneously. Bring the ball back beside your hip and step forward with the opposite foot, bending your knees into a semi-crouch position (Step 1). If you're passing the ball from your right hip, step forward with your left foot and vice versa.

At the end of this backswing your right hand is slightly behind your left and your right elbow is cocked back behind you (Step 2). From here both hands bring the ball forward, rotating the ball slightly until, when the ball is just in front of you, your hands are even—neither is very much ahead of the other. As you swing the ball forward, your weight starts forward too (Step 3).

Both hands follow the ball all the way out and the ball leaves both hands simultaneously (Step 4). Follow through with

Step 3

Step 4

Step 5

both hands extended and your weight fully forward, leaning into the pass. Let the ball slide off the ends of your fingers naturally (Step 5).

The two-handed underhand pass is a simple movement, useful as a hand-off or for short, quick passes. You should be able to perform it well, from either the right hip or the left.

You'll need skill in passing from both sides to elude guards working close to you.

This one-hand underhand pass is exactly the same as the two-hand underhand pass, except that during the forward swing the right hand stays behind the ball. The left comes away and only the right hand follows through.

1-HAND UNDERHAND PASS

Step 1

Step 2

Up to the end of the backswing, it is exactly the same as the two-hand underhand pass (Step 1). Now as the forward swing starts, the left hand stays in front, leading the swing until the ball is just in front of the body. At this point, the left hand leaves the ball entirely and swings off to the left while the right hand stays behind the ball, pushing it forward toward the receiver (Step 2). The follow-through is with the right hand only—the arm fully extended and the weight well forward on the left foot (Step 3). Of course, the left hand can be used alone in the one-hand underhand pass just as well as the right.

Step 3

BOUNCE PASS

The bounce pass is a method of getting the ball past guards where other passes would be blocked. You simply bounce the ball to the receiver instead of throwing it. This pass should start from an underhand or low chest position because a higher starting position would increase the distance the ball has to travel, thus giving your opponent more time to block it.

In Step 1 a bounce pass is developing out of what started as a two-hand underhand pass. All the fundamentals are the same until the ball is just in front of you on the forward swing. But now,

Step 1

Step 2

instead of passing straight out in front of you, change direction slightly and bounce the ball to the receiver (Step 2). This type of pass requires more finger control than ordinary push passes.

There are many other types of passes in basketball—for instance, a hook pass—but those we have discussed are the basic passes. Learn and practice those well, and the others will come to you easily and naturally when you are ready for them.

52

4. Dribbling

So far we have emphasized the basic techniques of good control of the ball—so essential to playing winning basketball. Now with dribbling, it's time to learn the second fundamental basketball skill—control of the body in possession of the ball. For only with perfect poise and constant body balance is the dribbler able to maintain possession of the ball against alert opposition.

Step 1

Step 2

Dribbling is basically an arm-wrist-finger action. The starting position is shown in Step 1—your body bent slightly forward, knees relaxed, your forearm parallel with the floor and your arm as relaxed as possible. From this position, move your forearm upward about 5 inches, with fingers and wrist well relaxed (Step 2), then back down about 12 inches. Keep your upper arm steady, moving your forearm on the elbow joint with your fingers and wrist relaxed (Step 3).

Step 3

54

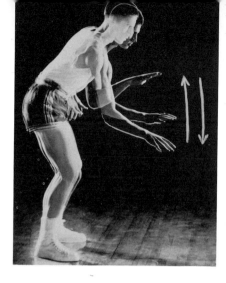

Step 4

Step 4 shows the whole dribble movement—easy, relaxed, up and down with a relaxed but controlled wrist. It isn't a slapping movement—more of a pushing down with spread fingers and drawing back up again. Practice this movement until it feels smooth and rhythmic with each hand. Then, using the same relaxed motion, start bouncing the ball on the floor (Step 5). Don't slap the ball down, just push it down and let your hand ride back up with it. After the downward push hold your hand down and wait for the ball. Then let your fingers and hand ride back up with it (Step 6).

Step 5

Step 6

Step 7   Step 8

Now simply push it back down again (Step 7). Your fingers should be in contact with the ball for as long as possible during the upward and downward movements. That way you keep better control.

Try the same thing with your other hand (Step 8), and practice the dribble until you have perfect control with both hands and without looking at the ball. Focus your eyes on the floor a few feet in front of you.

When you've mastered the dribble standing still, start moving forward, dribbling as you go. Try to keep your eyes off the ball. If you look at the ball, you cannot see what the other players are doing. Move slowly at first (Step 1).

Step 1

| *Step 2* | *Step 3* |

Notice that now, instead of pressing the ball straight down, you have to push it slightly forward to keep it ahead of your moving body (Step 2). When you can walk slowly forward and dribble without looking at the ball, change hands and master the dribble with the other hand (Step 3). Don't try to travel fast until the coordination of your legs and arm is completely natural.

It should be apparent, however, that while you are in an upright position, the ball is relatively unprotected. It would be easy for an opposing guard to snatch it away from you as it makes that long trip from your hand to the floor.

Step 1

To protect the ball better, keep low—shorten the distance between your hand and the floor. Without the ball, crouch low like a sprinter at the start of a race (Step 1), and practice moving around with your body close to the floor (Step 2).

Step 2

Step 3

Then, keeping your body low, try dribbling. In this position, with your hand working so close to your knees, you'll have to be particularly careful about the distance you keep the ball ahead of you (Step 3).

If you dribble too close, the ball will hit your knees, bounce away, and you'll lose it (Photo 1). If you dribble too far ahead

Photo 1

Photo 2

of you it will be difficult to control (Photo 2). Through practice you'll find the best distance between you and the ball at all speeds and in all body positions.

As you gain skill and start to pick up speed, raise your body higher from the crouched position, provided you're in the clear (Photo 3). But when you're threatened drop back to the crouch position, because that way you have the best protection (Photo 4).

Photo 3

Photo 4

Photo 5

Photo 5 shows how your hunched-over body protects that ball. And the shorter the distance the ball has to travel from your hand to the floor, the less the danger of losing it to an opponent.

Keep both arms well in front of you. You'll find a tendency to let the arm not being used for dribbling drop down to the side. But keep it up and ahead of you (Photo 6). You'll need it to

Photo 6

Photo 7

ward off opponents and to recover the ball if it should be knocked out of your control (Photo 7).

In dribbling, as in passing, wide-angle vision will be one of your most valuable assets. With good wide-angle vision, you should be able to identify players at almost 90 degrees from your forward direction. If you look in the direction you're going to move, you signal your intention and you'll probably be blocked (Photo 8).

Photo 8

Photo 9

But if you keep your eyes on the floor in front of you, just over the top of your working hand, you'll be able to see openings and teammates without looking at them and your opponents will never know your next move (Photo 9).

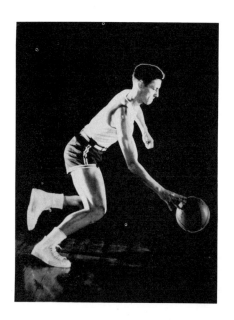

Dribbling is one of basketball's essential skills. All it takes is a knowledge of the fundamentals, and plenty of practice.

5. Pivoting

One of the important maneuvers, one that helps make basketball such a highly competitive sport, is the pivot, which gives the offensive player a means of meeting and avoiding the defensive tactics of an energetic guard. To pivot, come to a stop and swing around on one foot, then either shoot for the basket, dribble, or pass to a teammate to get the ball out of

danger. The main thing is to protect the ball by placing your body between the ball and opposing guard.

A pivoting player is much like a pair of proportional dividers. Just as dividers pivot on one of their two points and swing through complete circles (Photo 1), so a basketball player

Photo 1

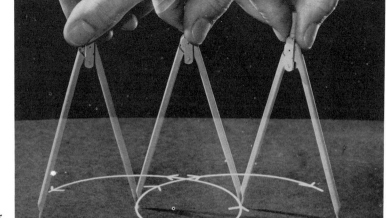

Photo 2

pivots on one or the other foot, through a complete circle or as much of the circle as he wants, without lifting that pivot foot off the floor (Photo 2). The rules define legal and illegal pivots, so let's examine them first.

The simplest pivot rule applies to a player who receives the ball while standing still with both feet on the floor (Photo 3).

Photo 3

Photo 4

That man may pivot in either direction on his left foot (Photo 4) or in either direction on his right foot (Photo 5). He has his choice.

But supposing that player caught the ball while moving

Photo 5

Photo 6

with one foot in the air and decided to pivot before either passing or shooting. He would have to come to a stop when that foot in the air touched the ground (Photo 6). That's called a two-count stop—when you receive the ball with one foot in the air. Count one as you catch the ball, and two as your foot comes to the ground (Photo 7).

2-COUNT STOP

Photo 7

Photo 8

On a two-count stop your rear foot *must* be your pivot foot
(Photo 8), and you can pivot around on that foot as long as you
want to, as long as you don't lift that pivot foot off the floor
(Photo 9).

Photo 9

Photo 10

Photos 10 and 11 show an exception to the two-count stop rule. This is a two-count stop, but the lifted foot came down exactly parallel with the first one. In this case, you can pivot on either foot, just as if you had caught the ball standing still with both feet on the ground.

In Photo 12 is another type of stop—a one-count stop. The player caught the ball while he was in the air, with both feet

Photo 11

1-COUNT STOP

Photo 12

off the ground. Both feet come down together in a single count
after he caught the ball. In this case he can pivot on either foot
just as though he had been standing still. Those are the basic
rules of pivoting.

Now let's see how to use these pivots and turns in play.
Photo 13 shows a reverse pivot, in which you pivot back, away
from your opponent. As you meet your opponent in this situa-

Photo 13

Step 1

tion, the ball is exposed. If you pass to the right or left, the chances are he'll be able to reach the ball. So you decide to pivot and pass to the right (Step 1).

Your right foot is your pivot foot and you swing your body back around to the left. Now your shoulder is coming between the ball and your opponent (Step 2). Keep swinging around to

Step 2

Step 3

the left until your back is to your opponent, with your whole body between him and the ball (Step 3), and pass, using your body for protection (Step 4).

Step 4

Step 1

In the same situation you can protect the ball with your shoulder by using a forward cross or turn. In Step 1 you receive the ball with your feet parallel, so you can pivot on either foot. You can swing your left foot forward and across in front of you, bringing your shoulder between your opponent and the ball (Step 2). Then you can pass to the right.

Or you can swing your right foot across in front of you (Step

Step 2

Step 3

3), and pass off to the left (Step 4). Pivots, crosses and turns like this can get you out of trouble quickly and they can often open the way for an offensive play.

A pivot is most useful when it is performed with speed and deception. So learn the fundamentals and then practice them thoroughly so that they become an instinctive part of your body control and ball handling during a game.

Step 4

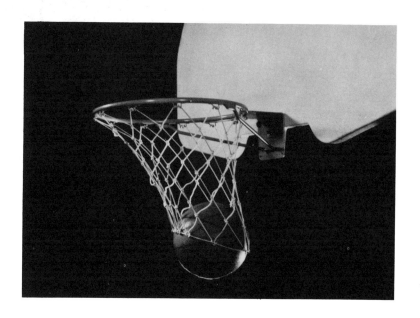

6. Shooting

All fundamental skills in basketball are important to the game. But if any one were to be singled out for extra practice, it would be the fundamentals of shooting. It's the ability to shoot, to see the ball sink through the basket on a good percentage of shots that wins games.

It makes little difference how well a team dribbles and passes, how it works the ball into scoring position, unless every player on the team can score baskets. Let's analyze the fundamentals of some of the most common shots.

One is the chest or push shot, used mostly for long-range shooting. Essentially the shot uses the same movements as the

chest or push pass—a short downward and backward swing with bent knees to get the movement flowing smoothly, then an upward push toward the basket as the knees straighten and push upward simultaneously. Then a forward step for the follow-through.

When you are far out on the floor and closely guarded, the swing is longer and you need to jump straight up as you push upwards. This allows you to release the ball over your opponent's head and land with your feet together. Called the jump shot, this is a variation of the chest shot.

CHEST OR PUSH SHOT

Step 1

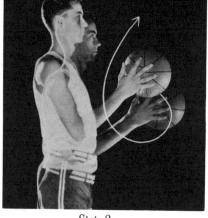

Step 2

Step 1 is your starting position — ball about chest high, lightly but firmly cushioned in the fingers and thumbs, not against the palms. Eyes should be on the target and they must stay there until the ball reaches its destination. Now start the shot with a downward movement.

Swing the ball down and back in a small smooth loop (Step 2). The purpose of this preliminary swing is to get the ball in motion smoothly and avoid a sudden push, which makes control more difficult. Simultaneously bend your knees.

Don't move your feet. Just sink your hips slightly to get your body down behind the upward swing (Step 3). Now continue

Step 3

Step 4

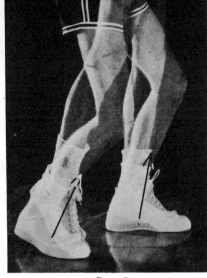

Step 5

the preliminary swing by pushing the ball upward toward the basket in a high looping arc (Step 4). Push with your arms and with your knees to get the power of your legs into the shot. Your rear foot will come completely off the floor during the shot (Step 5).

Continue the arm movement, pushing—not throwing—the ball on its way. Follow through with your arms outstretched and your palms toward the basket (Step 6).

Step 6

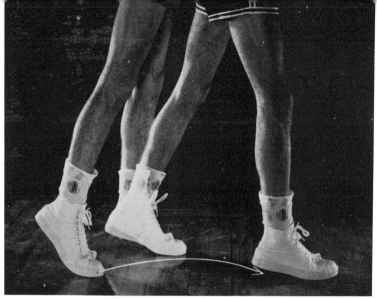

Step 7

Now, as your weight comes forward with the shot, bring your rear foot forward in a short step to keep your balance (Step 7), and end in an alert position ready to go in after the rebound if necessary (Step 8).

The one-hand chest or push shot is a variation of the two-hand shot. Footwork is exactly the same. The difference comes

Step 8

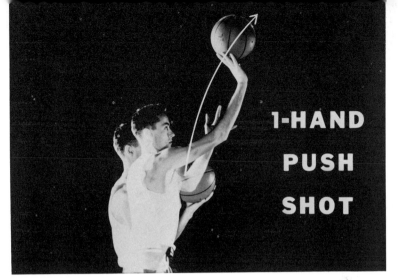

1-HAND PUSH SHOT

as the ball is carried up from the chest position when one hand drops away from the ball and the other pushes it on toward the basket and follows through.

From the catching position, the movement starts with the same short preliminary swing, down and back to get the action flowing smoothly (Step 1). But as the ball comes back up, rotate the ball between your hands to get one hand under the ball and the other behind it—the pushing hand behind and the other underneath. In Step 2 the shot will be a right-hand shot so your right hand is behind the ball and the left simply holds

Step 1

Step 2

81

Step 3

it in position. From here simply push with your right hand (Step 3). As your right hand gets control of the ball, let your left hand swing out to the side for balance and follow through after the ball (Step 4), just as in the two-hand push shot, except that here only the pushing hand follows through. Then prepare to go after any rebound.

Step 4

LAY-UP
SHOT

Another valuable shot is the lay-up, or under-the-basket shot, made while you are charging in to score. Simply move toward the basket, leap into the air at a point where your forward momentum will carry you almost under it—but to one side. Lay the ball up against the backboard about 18 inches above the rim, from which spot it should carom into the basket.

Since footwork is the important factor here, let's practice it first. If you are approaching the basket from the right side, run in and take off from your left foot (Step 1).

Step 1

Step 2

This puts the body in a natural throwing position for shooting with your right hand, which is the hand to use on the right side of the basket. By using the hand closest to the backboard, you protect the ball (Step 2).

Now practice coming into the left side of the basket and leaping on your right foot (Step 3). Now your left hand is in a

Step 3

Step 4

free position to swing the ball upward (Step 4). The rule to remember is "Opposite foot, opposite hand."

Now practice dribbling with the ball toward the right side of the basket, or practice catching a pass near the basket. With the ball held in both hands, about waist high, start your jump, bringing the ball upward as you do so (Step 1).

Step 1

Step 2

With both hands, push the ball upward as far as possible (Step 2). Then at the full extent of both arms, let the left hand drop away. Push the ball upward with your right, laying it against the board about 18 inches above the rim (Step 3). The ball should then carom back through the basket.

Now practice the same basic movements, but approach the basket from the left side, leap from the floor with your right foot and shoot with your left hand. In all cases, this should be a graceful, easy-flowing movement (Step 4).

Step 3

Step 4

Step 5

If you approach the basket directly from the front, don't try to lay it against the board but on an imaginary shelf about 18 inches above the front portion of the rim, so that the ball drops through the rim without touching the backboard (Step 5).

A basic shot that every player should learn is the pivot or hook shot. As you receive the ball with your back to the basket, turn to your left, spot the basket quickly, and lay the ball up against the backboard with your right hand.

PIVOT OR HOOK SHOT

Step 1

Start the motion with the ball held in approximate receiving position. Your feet will usually be parallel to each other (Step 1). In play you may want to draw your guard off balance with a feint to the right, but your first shooting movement is to your left with your left foot—a step around toward the basket as your body starts to pivot (Step 2).

Step 2

Step 3

Next, shift your weight to your left foot, as you swing your body around to the left (Step 3). At almost the same moment, spot the basket and bring the ball up in a wide, over-the-head sweeping movement. Shoot to lay the ball against the backboard (Step 4).

Step 4

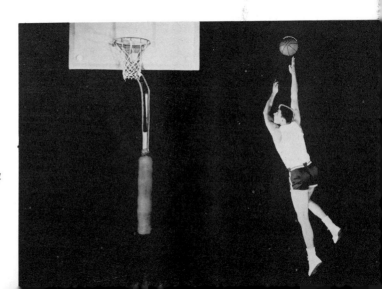

Step 5

As your body carries around to face the basket, your weight comes back into balance on both feet (Step 5). Naturally this shot may be made by turning right instead of left, and using the left hand after shifting your weight to your right foot.

Many basketball games are won by the free throw from the foul line, so every player should learn its fundamentals and be able to use them well. This shot is usually made with a two-hand underhand or pull motion from a position directly behind the foul line. The toe of the forward foot should be placed about an inch back from the foul line (Step 1), although you may find it more comfortable to stand with feet parallel.

For an accurate free throw, the ball must be centered in your hands. Find the center spot by spinning the ball between your two index fingers, guiding its motion with your thumbs. When the ball twirls evenly, without pulling in any direction, you will have found the exact center (Step 2). Now spread your fingers

Step 1

Step 2

Step 3   Step 4

evenly around the ball, a little to the rear of center. In this spot, more than in any of the others, the muscles of arms and hands must be thoroughly relaxed, except for what pressure is necessary to hold the ball (Step 3).

Now you are ready to make the throw. As you get set, you may be conscious of extreme nervous tension. A deep breath, held for a few seconds, will help in slowing down the heart action and calming your nerves (Step 4). Begin the throwing motion by bending your knees in a slight crouch. With your arms straight, drop the ball to a position between your knees. Your weight should rest on the balls of your feet (Step 5).

Now bring the ball upward with your arms in a wide,

Step 5

Step 6   *Step 7*

extended arc, and at the same time rise up from your crouch (Step 6). On the follow-through take a long upward and slightly forward stretch after the ball. The palms should be facing inward and forward, hands about a foot apart (Step 7). The ball should travel in a medium and constant arc to the basket, and drop through the rim (Step 8).

There is no easy road to accurate shooting. You may be a born shooter, with natural body control that will go a long way toward making you an accurate marksman. But practice alone will give you the confidence to be able to shoot well consistently under game pressure.

Step 8

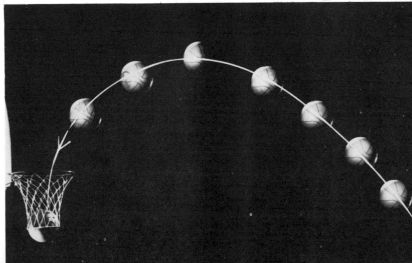

7. Defense

So far in this series we have studied the techniques of advancing the ball and scoring. In other words, we have studied offense. But offense is only half of the game. Of equal importance are the techniques of defense, for no matter how fast and accurate your team may be, your score won't win for you unless you keep your opponents from scoring as well or better. There are three strategic types of defense.

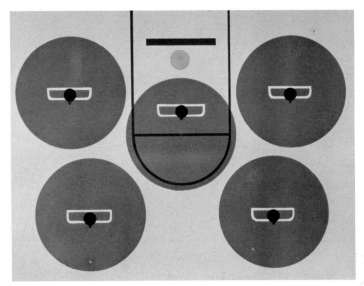

Illus. 1

First, there is zone defense, in which each player is responsible for a certain zone on the floor and each player guards any opponent who enters his zone (Illus. 1). Second, there is man-to-man or individual defense. Here each player is assigned a certain opposing player and he guards that player no matter where he goes on the floor (Illus. 2). There are many combinations of these two systems but they are all just variations of these two basic plans.

Illus. 2

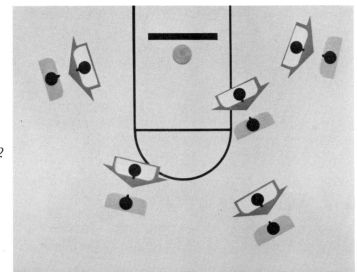

No matter what types of defense your team uses, success depends on how well each player does his individual job. We can learn best by studying man-to-man defense.

The best stance for defense is the one that gives you the greatest mobility. Be ready to move in any direction instantly, and try to make your arms and body cover as great an area as possible.

Photo 1

Start practicing the stance by placing your feet like a boxer's —one foot slightly ahead of the other, feet well spread and your weight well up on the balls of your feet (Photo 1). Then bend your knees, let your hips sink and spread your arms wide. You can keep your arms extended sideways, as shown in Photo 2, if you wish.

Photo 2

Photo 3

This sideways spread gives your opponent an impression of a very wide obstacle to go around, and from here you can raise or lower your arms to offset any tactics he may use (Photo 3). Or, in some instances, you may want to have one hand up and the other out to the side (Photo 4).

The advantage of this position is that your upraised hand is

Photo 4

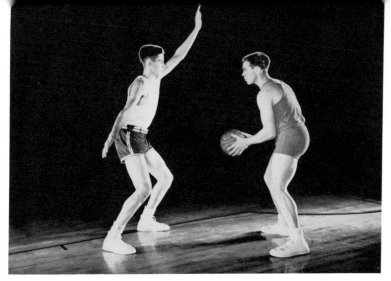

Photo 5

ready to block overhead shots or passes, while the other is in position to thrust at the ball or block low passes (Photo 5). If you use this stance you should practice alternating hands so that you can guard just as effectively with either hand held up.

The third effective arm position is with both hands out in front below shoulder height. This is probably the most natural of the three (Photo 6). In this position you can make catlike

Photo 6

Photo 7

thrusts at the ball, and raise or lower your hands quickly if your opponent passes (Photo 7).

You'll probably use all three positions at different times, so be proficient in all of them. But whatever your position, keep moving. Keep your arms moving and move your body to present as difficult an obstacle as possible. A moving guard

distracts a player and makes it difficult for him to concentrate on his passing or shooting. So keep moving.

A guard's footwork is like the footwork of a boxer. Always keep your feet apart and don't walk or run when you're guarding close—shuffle with short, quick steps (Photo 8).

Photo 8

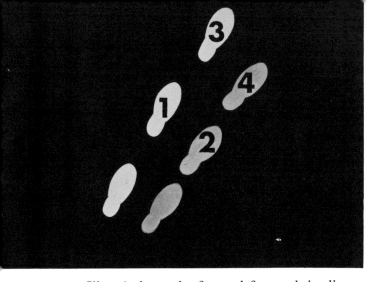

Illus. 1

Illus. 1 shows the forward footwork in diagram form. The forward foot moves forward first. Then the rear foot comes up behind. Then the front foot forward again, and the rear foot up behind. You never cross your legs and your forward foot stays forward.

To move backward, simply reverse the process. First your rear foot slides back, then your front foot comes back after it. Then the rear foot again, and then the front foot (Illus. 2).

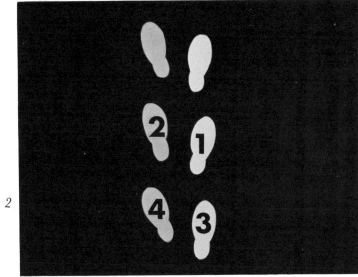

Illus. 2

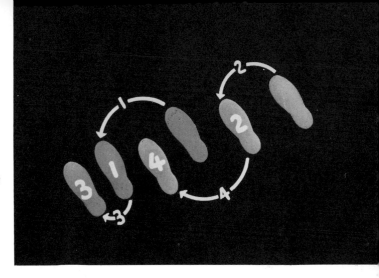

Illus. 3

To move sideways, it's the same shuffle. If you want to move to the left, your left foot moves first; then the right foot follows (Illus. 3). In defensive basketball, never cross your legs.

You may be tempted to take a running step to catch up with a fast player, but if you do and your opponent suddenly changes direction, you're off balance and you'll probably be left two or three steps behind (Photo 1).

Photo 1

Photo 2

Don't lunge or take long steps toward your opponent, as shown in Photo 2. A smart offensive player will make his break or cut around you while you are in the middle of the lunge. Before you can recover you've lost him.

Ideally your job on defense is to prevent your opponent from getting any closer to the basket than when he receives the ball. The only way you can do this is to confront him with an

Photo 3

Photo 4

obstacle to his forward progress, so your best position on defense is between your opponent and his basket (Photo 3).

When he comes toward you with the ball you must decide whether to rush in and meet him or wait for him to come to you (Photo 4). If he's coming in at full speed, drop back toward the basket and get started in the same direction he's coming (Photo 5). At the same time try to crowd him toward the sideline and, if possible, force him out of bounds.

Photo 5

Photo 6

But if he's approaching slowly go out and meet him, arms outstretched, and block his progress (Photo 6). He'll very likely try to go around you, first feinting one way to throw you off balance and then cutting around you in the opposite direction (Photo 7).

Photo 7

Photo 8

To get around you he'll have to travel in a wide arc. The temptation for you will be to try to follow close beside him in a smaller arc of your own (Photo 8). However, this would be a mistake.

What you should do is break in a straight line for a spot that will put you between the dribbler and the basket.

Here the dribbler, represented by the solid line, cuts in a wide arc. The guard (dotted line) cuts straight toward a point where he can meet the dribbler again and place an obstacle in his path toward the basket.

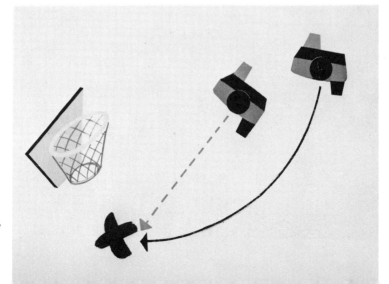

Photo 9

Photo 10

If you do this, in most cases your opponent will be forced to stop and either pass back or shoot under great difficulty (Photo 9).

Occasionally, you may feel in a position to bat the ball away from the dribbler. But you will find that in most cases the effort will throw you off balance and out of step so that the dribbler will be able to get around you (Photo 10).

You will find that if you simply concentrate on keeping your proper defensive position—that is, between the dribbler and his basket—you will be doing enough. After the dribbler has been stopped, he can only pass or shoot, and you should be in a position to interfere with either movement (Photo 11).

Photo 11

Photo 12

When the player you are guarding does not have the ball, still maintain your defensive position between him and the basket although you may play him "loose"—that is you don't have to stay as close to him as you do when he has the ball. This "loose" position gives you a better chance to see both the opponent *and* the ball (Photo 12). And when the ball comes toward your man, you can move in quickly (Photo 13).

Photo 13

In team play other offensive men may interfere with your defense so you must be aware of actions of other offensive players as well. You must also be ready to take the offense whenever the opportunity presents itself. Your most likely chance for recovering the ball, aside from fumbles, is in taking rebounds off the backboard. Hence your rebound position is all-important. When your opponent shoots for the basket, prepare to screen him from following his shot (Step 1). Don't turn to

Step 1

Step 2   Step 3

face the basket immediately, but watch him until he shows what direction he will take (Step 2). Then turn to block him out, pick up the flight of the ball and go in after it (Step 3).

As we said before, the key to all success in defensive play is mental alertness. Because the defensive player cannot know what action to expect from his opponent, he must be ready for anything. But after all, that's one of the things that makes basketball one of the nation's favorite sports.

SOME RULES OF BASKETBALL

The Playing Area

Basketball may be played indoors or out of doors, although in America it is generally an indoor game. Basketball is played on a court ranging in size from a maximum of 94 feet long by 50 feet wide to a minimum of 74 feet long by 42 feet wide. Ideal measurements are:

College Age	94 by 50 feet
High School Age	84 by 50 feet
Junior High School Age	74 by 42 feet

The court is to have a hard surface, usually of wood. There should at least be 3 feet (preferably 10) of unobstructed space on all sides of the court.

At either end of the court there are backboards made of wood, glass, steel or other rigid, flat materials. The backboards must be one of two types: a rectangle 6 feet long and 4 feet high, or a fan-shaped board. The front face of the backboard is to be four feet in from the end boundary line, and parallel with it. The basket is attached to the center of the backboard so that the rim of the basket is 10 feet from the floor. From the basket ring is suspended a white cord net.

In the exact center of the court is a circle, 4 feet in diameter, known as the center circle. A "restraining circle," 12 feet in diameter, is concentric with the center circle.

At the center at each end of the court there are free-throw lanes, 12 feet wide, ending in circles 12 feet in diameter. The centers of these circles are to be 19 feet from the end boundary lines. A "free-throw line" is drawn through the circle, parallel with the end boundary line. The free-throw line is 15 feet from the plane of the face of the backboard.

A "division line" divides the court into two equal parts. A team's "front court" is that part of the court containing the team's own basket, that is, the basket through which a team tries to score its points. The other half of the court is known as that team's "back court." For an opposing team, the names are reversed.

The Ball

A basketball is to be round, no larger than 30 inches in circumference and no smaller than 29. Its weight should be no more than 22 ounces nor less than 20 ounces. When inflated, it should bounce to a height (measured to top of ball) of not less than 49 inches nor more than 54 inches after it has been dropped from a height of six feet (measured to bottom of ball). The home team is to provide the basketball for any game.

The Team

A basketball team consists of 5 players, generally known as a center, two forwards and two guards. A team cannot begin a game with less than five players, but if it has no substitutes to replace disqualified players, it must finish the game with less than five players. Under current rules, a player must leave the game after committing five personal fouls, and cannot return during that game. Each player should wear a numbered shirt.

The Officials

The officials should be a Referee and an Umpire, assisted by two Timers and two Scorers. A single Timer and a single Scorer may be used if acceptable to both teams. Officials must conduct the game according to the rules.

Scorers record personal and technical fouls, and notify the Referee when the fifth personal foul is called on a player. They also record time-outs charged against each team. In keeping track of the scoring, most officials use the following symbols:

P1, P2, P3, etc. for personal fouls;

T for technical fouls;

O for free throw attempt, X inside the O if try is good;

2 for field goals.

A field goal counts two points. A successful free throw counts 1 point.

Game Times

Teams of college age play two 20-minute halves, with a 15-minute intermission between the halves.

Teams of high school age play four 8-minute quarters, with two 1-minute intermissions between the quarters and a 10-minute intermission between the halves.

For teams of less than high school age, the quarters are 6 minutes, with 2-minute intermissions between quarters and a 10-minute intermission at half time.

Overtime Periods

If the score is tied at the end of the second half in games of college-age levels, play shall continue for an extra period of 5 minutes, or for as many extra 5-minute periods as are needed to break the tie. A 2-minute intermission is taken before each extra period. The ball is put in play at the center circle at the start of each extra period.

In games of high school age level or below, games which end in ties at the end of regulation time are played off in extra periods of 3 minutes each, with a 2-minute intermission before each extra period. If a team is ahead by 1 point or more at the end of any extra period, it wins. As soon as a team accumulates 2 points after the first extra period, the game is immediately over, and that team wins.

Time-Outs

Each team is allowed five charged time-outs during regular play. A charged time-out is either a time-out requested by a player when the ball is dead or that player's team has control of the ball; or a time-out for an injury or removal of a disqualified player, except that a time-out is not charged if an injured or disqualified player is replaced within $1\frac{1}{2}$ minutes. If the officials halt a game to permit a player to tie a shoelace, a time-out is not charged.

Some Other Rules

Visiting teams have the choice of baskets for the first half. Teams change baskets for the second half.

The score of a forfeited game is 2 to 0.

When a team gains control of the basketball in its back court, it must move the ball into its front court within 10 seconds, unless the ball is touched by an opponent. When that happens, a new play starts, with a new 10-second period allowed.

SOME COMMON BASKETBALL TERMS

ADVANCING FIGURE OF EIGHT: An attempt by ball handlers to move the ball toward the basket, following a figure-eight pattern.

BANK SHOT: A shot off the backboard.

BASKET-HANGING: Remaining under opponents' basket while opponents have the ball in other territory.

BLIND PASS: Looking in one direction and passing ball in another, using split vision.

BRUSH-OFF: Getting rid of a defensive player by forcing him to run into one of your teammates.

CAGE: To score a basket.

CLEAN SHOT: A shot that goes through the hoop without touching backboard.

CRIP SHOT: An easy short shot, close to basket, made without interference.

DECOY CUT: A cut calculated to free a teammate from being guarded.

DRAG: A dribble in which the ball is dribbled at the side of the body to keep it away from a guarding opponent.

FADE: To retreat to back court or defended basket.

FOLLOW-IN: A dash toward the basket to grab a rebound, should one result.

FOUL LINE NOTCH: The point where the free-throw lane meets the free-throw circle.

FREE PLAY: Slow deliberate offensive with much passing and faking, followed by a sudden concerted scoring effort should a defensive lapse occur. Also called "Eastern Style."

GIVE-AND-GO: Offensive player passes to teammate then cuts for basket to either take a long return pass or draw the defense out of position.

HOPE SHOT: A wild desperate shot at the basket, that has little chance of scoring.

JACKNIFE: The doubling action of the legs and body by a player taking a pass or a rebound from the backboard.

PICK-UP POINT: The part of the court where defensive men await their respective opponents and start a man-to-man defense against them.

REVERSE ROLL: Player fakes to go in front of a teammate, pivots, spins, and goes behind him.

SET SHOT: An unhurried long shot taken from a well-balanced position; usually a two-handed shot.

SHOVEL PASS: A short pass, one- or two-handed, in which the ball, from a point near the floor, is "shoveled" up to a teammate.

SWITCHING: A reversal of defensive positions. Players guarding certain opponents switch positions to guard other ones.

TIP-IN SHOT: A shot in which an offensive player tries to tip or deflect the ball, in the air and near the basket into, the basket.

OFFICIAL BASKETBALL SIGNALS

1 Start clock

2 Stop clock or do not start clock

3 Stop clock for jump ball

4 Beckon substitute when ball is dead and clock stopped

5 Stop clock for foul

6 Holding— follows Signal 5

7 Pushing or charging —follows Signal 5

8 Illegal use of hand —follows Signal 5

9 Technical foul

10 Blocking —follows Signal 5

11 No score

12 Goal counts or is awarded

13 Point(s) scored (1 or 2)

14 Bonus situation (for second throw drop one arm)

15 Traveling— Follow with Signal 18

16 Illegal dribble —follow with Signal 18

17 3-seconds violation —follow with Signal 18

18 Other violations also designates out of bounds spot and direction ball will go

19 Player Control Foul

For free throw violation: Use Signals 2 and 18

For basket interference: Use Signals 11 or 12 and 13

Basketball Rules

As adopted by the National Basketball Committee of the United States and Canada representing the National Collegiate Athletic Association, the National Federation of State High School Athletic Associations, the National Junior College Athletic Association, the Young Men's Christian Association, the Canadian Intercollegiate Athletic Union, and the Canadian Amateur Basketball Association.

Rule 1   Equipment

SECTION 1. The **playing court** shall be a rectangular surface free from obstructions and with dimensions not greater than 94 feet in length by 50 feet in width.

IDEAL MEASUREMENTS ARE:

High School Age..50 by 84 feet
College Age ....50 by 94 feet

SECTION 2. The **playing court** shall be marked with **sidelines, end lines** and other lines as shown on the **court diagram** (page 4). There shall be at least 3 feet (and preferably 10 feet) of unobstructed space outside.

If, on an unofficial court, there are less than 3 feet of unobstructed space outside any sideline or end line, a narrow broken line shall be marked in the court parallel with and 3 feet inside that boundary. This **restraining line** becomes the boundary line during a throw-in as in 7-6, on that side or end. It continues to be the boundary until the ball crosses the line.

NOTE—It is recommended that both players' benches be placed along that side of the court on which the scorers' table is located. Placing the players' benches outside the end lines should be discouraged.

SECTION 3. The **center circle** is a circle 2 inches in width and having a radius of 2 feet measured to the inside. A 2-inch wide circle concentric with the center circle shall be drawn with a radius of 6 feet measured to the outside.

SECTION 4. A **division line** 2 inches wide dividing the court into two parts shall be formed by extending the center circle diameter in both directions until it intersects the sidelines. If the court is less than 74 feet long, it should be divided by two lines, each parallel to and 40 feet from the farther end line.

SECTION 5. A **free throw lane**, 12 feet wide measured to the outside of each lane boundary and the semicircle with the free throw line as a diameter, shall be marked at each end of the court with dimensions and markings as shown on the court diagram. All bounding lines, but not lane space marks and neutral zone marks, are part of the lane. The color of the lane space marks and neutral zone marks shall contrast with the color of the bounding lines. The lane

118

space marks (2 inches by 8 inches) and neutral zone marks (12 inches by 8 inches) identify areas which extend from the outer edge of the lane lines 36 inches toward the sidelines.

SECTION 6. A free throw line, two inches wide, shall be drawn across each of the circles which have an outside radius of 6 feet as shown on the court diagram. It shall be parallel to the end line and shall have its farther edge 15 feet from the plane of the face of the backboard.

SECTION 7. Each of the two backboards shall be of any rigid material. The front surface shall be flat and, unless it is transparent, it shall be white. The backboard shall be either of two types: (1) A rectangle 6 feet horizontally and 4 feet vertically, or (2) a fan-shaped backboard, 54 inches wide and with dimensions as shown on the diagram.

If the backboard is transparent, it shall be marked as follows: A rectangle shall be centered behind the ring and marked by a 2-inch white line. The rectangle shall have outside dimensions of 24 inches

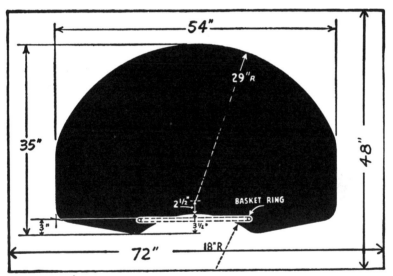

NOTE—Any backboard support, all of which is not directly behind the backboard, should be at least 6 inches behind it if the support extends above the top and at least 2 feet behind it if the support extends beyond the side. Attachment of ring to backboard shall be as prescribed in standards adopted by the Committee and available on request. For the fan-shaped backboard in transparent material, the recurved cut-out at the bottom may be filled in and the ring attached to the front of the backboard.

horizontally and 18 inches vertically. For the rectangular backboard, the top edge of the baseline shall be level with the ring. For the fan-shaped backboard, the baseline shall be omitted and the two vertical lines shall be extended to the bottom of the backboard. (The rectangular target in a bright orange color may be used on a non-transparent backboard.) The border of the backboard shall be marked with a white line. The border shall be 3 inches in width for the rectangular backboard and 3 inches or less in width for the fan-shaped backboard.

For college games, the transparent rectangular backboard shall be used. For other games, either type backboard in either transparent or non-transparent material is legal, but when new equipment is being installed for high school or Y.M.C.A. games, the fan-shaped backboard shall be used.

SECTION 8. Each backboard shall be midway between the sidelines, with the plane of its front face perpendicular to the floor, parallel to the end line and 4 feet from it. The upper edge of the backboard shall be: 13 feet above the floor for the rectangular and 12 feet 8 inches for the fan-shaped backboard.

SECTION 9. The backboards shall be protected from spectators to a distance of at least 3 feet at each end.

SECTION 10. Each basket shall consist of a metal ring, 18 inches in inside diameter, its flange and braces, and a white cord 12-mesh net, 15 to 18 inches in length, suspended from beneath the ring. Each ring shall be not more than ⅝ of an inch in diameter, with the possible addition of small-gauge loops on the under-edge for attaching a 12-mesh net. The ring and its attaching flange and braces shall be bright orange in color. The cord of the net shall be not less than 120-thread nor more than 144-thread seine twine, and shall be so constructed as to check the ball momentarily as it passes through.

SECTION 11. Each basket ring shall be securely attached to the backboard. It shall have its upper edge 10 feet above and parallel to the floor and shall be equidistant from the vertical edges of the backboard. The nearest point of the inside edge of the ring shall be 6 inches from the plane of the face of the backboard.

SECTION 12. The ball shall be spherical. Its color shall be the approved orange shade or natural tan. For college games, it shall have a leather cover unless the teams agree to use a ball with a composition cover. For high school or Y.M.C.A. games, it shall have a leather or composition cover. It shall be of the molded type. If the panels are leather, they shall be cemented to the spherically molded fabric which surrounds an air-tight rubber lining. Its circumference shall be within a maximum of 30 inches and a minimum of 29½ inches for adults and within a maximum of 29½ inches and a minimum of 29 inches for players below senior high school age. Its weight shall be not less than 20 nor more than 22 ounces. It shall be inflated to an air pressure such that when it is dropped to a solid wood floor from a height of six feet, measured to the bottom of the ball, it will rebound to a height, measured to the top of the ball, of not less than 49 inches when it strikes on its least resilient spot nor more than 54 inches when it strikes on its most resilient spot.

NOTE—To be legal, a ball must be tested for resilience at the factory and the air pressure which will give the required reaction must be stamped on it. The pressure for game use must be such as to make the ball bounce legally.

SECTION 13. The home team shall provide a ball which meets the specifications of section 12. If the ball is not legal, the referee may select for use a ball provided by the visiting team.

Rule 2 Officials and Their Duties

SECTION 1. The officials shall be a referee and an umpire, who shall be assisted by two timers and by two scorers. A single timer and a single scorer may be used if they are trained men acceptable to the referee.

NOTE—The officials should wear uniforms distinct from those of either team.

SECTION 2. The referee shall inspect and approve all equipment, including court, baskets, ball, backboards, timers' and scorers' signals. Prior to the scheduled starting time of the game, he shall designate the official timepiece, its operator, the official scorebook and official scorer. He shall be responsible for notifying each captain 3 minutes before each half is to begin.

The referee shall not permit any player to wear equipment which, in his judgment, is dangerous to other players. Elbow, hand, finger, wrist or arm guard, cast or brace made of sole leather, plaster, metal or any other hard substance, even though covered with soft padding, shall always be declared illegal.

Any equipment, which is unnatural and designed to increase a player's height or reach or to gain an advantage, shall not be used.

SECTION 3. The referee shall toss the ball at center to start the game. He shall decide whether a goal shall count if the officials disagree. He shall have power to forfeit a game when conditions warrant. He shall decide matters upon which the timers and the scorers disagree. At the end of each half he shall check and approve the score. His approval at the end of the game terminates the jurisdiction of the officials.

SECTION 4. The referee shall have power to make decisions on any points not specifically covered in the rules.

SECTION 5. The officials shall conduct the game in accordance with the rules. This includes: notifying the captains when play is about to begin at the start of the game, following an intermission or charged time-out, or after any unusual delay in putting the ball in play; putting the ball in play; determining when the ball becomes dead; prohibiting practice during a dead ball, except between halves; administering penalties; ordering time-out; beckoning substitutes to enter the court; warning a team for lack of sufficient action; signaling the point value of a goal by raising one or two fingers to face level and silently counting seconds to administer rules 4-11, 7-6, 8-4, 9-1, 9-7, 9-8, and 10-1-(c).

SECTION 6. The officials shall penalize unsportsmanlike conduct by any player, coach, substitute, team attendant or follower. If there is flagrant misconduct, the officials shall penalize by removing any offending player from the game and banishing any offending coach, substitute, team attendant or follower from the vicinity of the court. A player who commits his fifth personal foul shall also be removed from the game.

SECTION 7. Neither official shall have authority to set aside or question decisions made by the other within the limits of his respective outlined duties.

121

SECTION 8. The officials shall have power to make decisions for infractions of rules committed either within or outside the boundary lines; also at any moment from 10 minutes before the scheduled starting time of the game to the referee's approval of the final score. This includes the periods when the game may be momentarily stopped for any reason.

SECTION 9. (a) When a foul occurs, an official shall signal the timer to stop his watch and he shall designate the offender to the scorers and indicate with his fingers the number of free throws. The offending player shall raise his hand at arm's length above his head.

(b) When a team is entitled to a throw-in, an official shall clearly signal the act which caused the ball to become dead, the throw-in spot unless it follows a successful goal or an awarded goal, and the player or team entitled to the throw-in. The official shall hand (not toss) the ball to the thrower-in for a throw-in unless the throw-in is from outside an endline following a successful goal.

SECTION 10. Officials may correct an error if a rule is inadvertently set aside and results in: (a) failure to award a merited free throw; or (b) awarding an unmerited free throw; or (c) permitting a wrong player to attempt a free throw; or (d) attempting a free throw at the wrong basket; or (e) erroneously counting or canceling a score. If such error is made while the clock is stopped, it must be recognized before the clock is next started. If the error is made while the clock is running, it must be recognized before the second live ball after the error.

If the error is a free throw by the wrong player, or at the wrong basket or the awarding of an unmerited free throw, the free throw and the activity during it, other than unsportsmanlike conduct, shall be canceled. However, other points scored, consumed time and additional activity, which may occur prior to the recognition of a mistake, shall not be nullified. Errors because of free throw attempts by the wrong player or at the wrong basket shall be corrected by applying rule 8-1 and 2.

If an error, which occurs while the clock is running, is corrected, play shall be resumed from the point at which it was interrupted to rectify the error.

NOTE—Having more than five squad members participating simultaneously, or participating after having been notified that he is disqualified, or a player participating after changing his number, without reporting it to the scorers and an official, are infractions which shall also be penalized if discovered during the time a provision is being violated. (See penalty following Rule 10, Sec. 7.)

SECTION 11. The scorers shall record the field goals made, the free throws made and missed, and shall keep a running summary of the points scored. They shall record the personal and technical fouls called on each player and shall notify the referee immediately when the fifth personal foul is called on any player. They shall record the time-outs charged to each team, and shall notify a team and its coach through an official whenever that team takes a fifth charged time-out. They shall signal the nearer official each time a team is granted a charged time-out in excess of the legal number and when a player commits a common foul after his team has been charged with its 4th or 6th personal foul during the half. The scorebook of the home team shall be the official book, unless the referee rules otherwise. The scorers shall compare their records after each goal, each foul and each charged time-out, notifying the referee at once of any discrepancy. If the error cannot be found, the referee shall accept the record of the official book, unless he has knowledge which permits him to decide otherwise. If the discrepancy is in the score and the error is not resolved, the referee shall accept the progressive team totals of the official scorebook.

The scorers shall keep a record of the names and number of players who are to start the game and of all substitutes who enter the game. When there is an infraction of the rules pertaining to submission of the roster, substitutions or numbers of players, they shall notify the nearer official.

The scorers shall use a horn or other device unlike that used by the officials or timers to signal the officials. This may be used immediately if (or as soon as) the ball is dead, or is in control of the offending team.

NOTE—The **Rules Committee** strongly recommends that the official scorer wear a **black and white striped garment** and that his location be clearly marked.

SECTION 12. The timers shall note when each half is to start and shall notify the referee more than three minutes before this time so that he may notify the teams, or cause them to be notified, at least three minutes before the half is to start. They shall signal the scorers three minutes before starting time. They shall record playing time and time of stoppages as provided in the rules.

The timers shall be provided with at least one stopwatch which shall be the game watch and which shall be operated by one of the timers, but so placed that both may see it.

The game watch shall be started as prescribed in rule 5-10.

Fifteen seconds before the expiration of an intermission, a charged time-out or a time-out for replacing a disqualified player, the timer shall sound a warning signal immediately after which the players shall be ready to resume play.

The game watch shall be stopped: at the expiration of time for each period, and when an official signals time-out as in 5-8. For a charged time-out, timers shall start a time-out watch and shall direct the scorers to signal the referee when it is time to resume play.

Expiration of playing time in each quarter, half or extra period shall be indicated by the timer's signal. This signal terminates player activity. If the timer's signal fails to sound, or is not heard, the timers shall go on the court or use other means to notify the referee immediately. If, in the meantime, a goal has been made or a foul has occurred, the referee shall consult the timers. If the timers agree that time expired before the ball was in flight, the goal shall not count. If they agree that the period ended (as in 5-6 (b)) before the foul occurred, the foul shall be disregarded unless it was unsportsmanlike. If the timers disagree, the goal shall count or the foul shall be penalized unless the referee has knowledge which alters such ruling.

NOTE—The use of an electric timing device is hereby authorized, together with such modifications in the foregoing as are essential to its operation. If two watches are used, one timer should operate the game watch and signal, and the other should serve as checker of the game watch and operator of the time-out watch.
  Ques.—Should timers tell players or coaches how much time remains? Ans.—On request of a captain, an official should give this information to both teams when the ball is dead and time is out.

Rule 3   Players and Substitutes

SECTION 1. **Each team** consists of 5 players, one of whom is the captain.

Ques.—May a team play with less than 5 players? Ans.—A team must begin with 5 players, but if it has no substitutes to replace disqualified players, it must continue with less than 5.

SECTION 2. **The captain** is the representative of his team and may address an official on matters of interpretation or to obtain essential information, if it is done in a courteous manner. Any player may address an official to request a time-out (5-8-Item 3) or permission to leave the court.

At least 10 minutes before scheduled starting time each team shall supply the scorers with name and number of each squad member who may participate.

At least 3 minutes before scheduled starting time each team shall designate its 5 starting players.

Failure to comply with either one of these provisions is a technical foul (team), unless the referee considers the failure unavoidable.

SECTION 3. **A substitute** who desires to enter shall report to the scorers, giving his name and number. If entry is at any time other than between halves, and a substitute, who is entitled and ready to enter, reports to the scorers before change of status of the ball is about to occur, the scorers shall sound the horn if (or as soon as) the ball is dead and time is out. The substitute shall remain outside the boundary until an official beckons him, whereupon he shall enter immediately. If the ball is about to become alive, the beckoning signal should be withheld. The entering player shall not replace a free thrower or a jumper except as stated in 6-3-c, d and e and 8-2 and 3. If he enters to replace a player who must jump or attempt a free throw, he shall withdraw until the next opportunity to substitute.

A player who has been withdrawn may not reenter before the next opportunity to substitute after the clock has started following his replacement.

Ques. (1)—When does a substitute become a player? Ans.—When he legally enters the court.

Ques. (2)—Following substitutions, should the official line up players to aid them in locating opponents? Ans.—This should be avoided if possible but may be done at the request of a captain when three or more substitutes for the same team enter during an opportunity to substitute.

SECTION 4. **Each player shall be numbered** on the front and back of his shirt with plain numbers of solid color contrasting with the color of his shirt, and made of material not less than ¾ inch wide. The number on the back shall be at least 6 inches high and that on the front at least 4 inches high. Neither of the single digit numbers (1) or (2) nor any digit greater than 5 shall be used, nor shall players on the same team wear identical numbers.

Ques. (1)—If contesting teams have suits of the same color, what shall be done? Ans.—If possible, each team should have two sets of suits, one of light color and the other dark. The light color is for home games. The team which violates this policy should change. If there is doubt, the officials should request the home team to change; on a neutral floor the officials decide.

Ques. (2)—What is the penalty for wearing an illegal number? Ans.—The penalty is a technical foul if the player enters the game, and the infraction is discovered before the clock starts, and if no penalty has been enforced against the player's team in that game for a like violation.

Ques. (3)—May the numbers on the shirt have a border? Ans.—Yes. However, the committee strongly recommends the border be no wider than ¼ inch.

124

Rule 4   Definitions

SECTION 1. A **basket** is the 18-inch ring, its flange and braces and appended net through which players attempt to throw the ball. A team's own basket is the one into which its players try to throw the ball. The visiting team shall have the irrevocable choice of baskets at which it may practice before the game and this basket shall be its choice for the 1st half. The teams shall change baskets for the 2nd half.

SECTION 2. **Blocking** is personal contact which impedes the progress of an opponent who does not have the ball.

SECTION 3. **Change of status** is the time at which a dead ball becomes alive or a live ball becomes dead. Change of status is about to occur when:
   a. A player has started to make a throw-in; or
   b. 80% of the time limit count has expired; or
   c. An official is ready to make the toss for a jump; or
   d. An official starts to place the ball at the disposal of a free thrower.

SECTION 4. A **player is in control** when he is holding a live ball or dribbling it.
   A **team is in control** when a player of the team is in control and also while a live ball is being passed between teammates. Team control continues until: the ball is in flight after a try for goal; or an opponent secures control; or the ball becomes dead. There is no team control: during a jump ball; a throw-in; during the tapping of a rebound; or after the ball is in flight following a try for goal. In these situations, team control is reestablished when a player secures control.

SECTION 5. A **disqualified player** is one who is barred from further participation in the game because of committing his fifth personal foul, or a flagrant foul, or for infraction of Rule 10-4 (a) or (b).

SECTION 6. A **dribble** is ball movement caused by a player in control who throws, bats or taps the ball in the air and/or throws, bats or pushes the ball to the floor and then catches it or touches it once or several times before catching it. The dribble ends when the dribbler: (a) catches the ball in one or both hands; or (b) touches the ball with both hands simultaneously; or (c) loses control as indicated in rules 4-4 and 9-5.
   An **air dribble** is that part of a dribble during which the dribbler throws or taps the ball in the air and then touches it before it touches the floor or is caught.

   Ques. (1)—Is a player dribbling while tapping the ball during a jump, or when a pass rebounds from his hand, or when he fumbles, or when he taps a rebound or a pass away from other players who are attempting to get it? **Ans.**—No. The player is not in control under these conditions.
   Ques. (2)—Is it a dribble when a player stands still and: (a) bounces the ball; or (b) holds the ball and touches it to the floor once or more? **Ans.**— (a) Yes. (b) No.
   Ques. (3)—May a dribbler alternate hands? **Ans.**—Yes.

SECTION 7. **Extra period** is the extension of playing time necessary to break a tie score.

SECTION 8. **a.** A **foul** is an infraction of the rules, the penalty for which is one or more free throws unless it is a double foul, or is a player control foul, in which case the free throw provision is cancelled. For convenience, a personal foul, which is neither flagrant nor intentional nor committed against a player trying for field goal, nor a part of a double or multiple foul, is termed a **common foul.**

b. A double foul is a situation in which two opponents commit personal fouls against each other at approximately the same time. A **false double foul** is a situation in which there are fouls by both teams, the second of which occurs before the clock is started following the first, but such that at least one of the attributes of a double foul is absent.

c. A flagrant foul is an unsportsmanlike act and may be a personal or technical foul of a violent or savage nature, or a technical noncontact foul, which displays vulgar or abusive conduct. It may or may not be intentional.

d. An intentional foul is a personal foul, which in the judgment of the official appears to be designed or premeditated. It is not based on the severity of the act.

e. A multiple foul is a situation in which two or more teammates commit personal fouls against the same opponent at approximately the same time. A **false multiple foul** is a situation in which there are two or more fouls by the same team and such that the last foul is committed before the clock is started following the first, and such that at least one of the attributes of a multiple foul is absent.

f. A personal foul (10-8) is a player foul which involves contact with an opponent while the ball is alive or after the ball is in possession of a player for a throw-in.

g. A player control foul is a common foul committed by a player while he or a teammate is in control.

h. A technical foul (10-1 to 7) is: a foul by a non-player, or a player foul which does not involve contact with an opponent, or a player foul which involves unsportsmanlike contact with an opponent while the ball is dead, except as indicated in last clause of (d) above.

i. An unsportsmanlike foul is a technical foul which consists of unfair, unethical or dishonorable conduct.

SECTION 9. A **free throw** is the privilege given a player to score one point by an unhindered try for goal from within the free throw circle and behind the free throw line. A free throw starts when the ball is given to the free thrower at the free throw line or is placed on the line. It ends when: the try is successful; or it is certain the try will not be successful; or when the try touches the floor or any player; or when the ball becomes dead.

SECTION 10. (a) A team's **front court** consists of that part of the court between its end line and the nearer edge of the division line and including its basket and the inbounds part of its backboard. A team's **back court** consists of the rest of the court including its opponents' basket and inbounds part of the backboard and the entire division line.

(b) A **live ball is in the front or back court** of the team in control as follows: (1) A ball which is in contact with a player or with the court is in the back court if either the ball or the player (either player if the ball is touching more than one) is touching the back court. It is in the front court if neither the ball nor the player is touching the back court. (2) A ball which is not in contact with a player or the court retains the same status as when it was last in contact with a player or the court.

Ques.—From the front court, A passes the ball across the division line. It touches a teammate who is in the air after leaping from the back court or it touches an official in the back court? Is the ball in the back court? **Ans.—** Yes. See 4-15.

SECTION 11. Held ball occurs when:

a. Opponents have hands so firmly on the ball that control cannot be obtained without undue roughness; or

b. A closely guarded player anywhere in his front court holds the ball for 5 seconds; or

c. A team, in its front court, controls the ball for 5 seconds in an area enclosed by screening teammates; or

d. In an attempt to consume time, a closely guarded player within a few feet of a front court boundary intersection dribbles, or combines dribbling and holding the ball for 5 seconds; or

e. In an attempt to consume time, a closely guarded player, in his mid-court area, dribbles, or combines dribbling and holding the ball for 5 seconds.

The player in control is closely guarded when his opponent is in a guarding stance at a distance not exceeding 6 feet from him.

Ques.—Is it a held ball merely because the player holding the ball is lying or sitting on the floor? **Ans.—**No.

SECTION 12. Holding is personal contact with an opponent which interferes with his freedom of movement.

SECTION 13. A **jump ball** is a method of putting the ball into play by tossing it up between two opponents in one of the three circles. It begins when the ball leaves the official's hand, and ends as outlined in rule 6-4.

SECTION 14. Lack of sufficient action is the failure of the responsible team to force play.

SECTION 15. The location of a player (or non-player) is determined by where he is touching the floor as far as being inbounds or out of bounds or being in the front court or back court is concerned. When he is in the air from a leap, his status with reference to these two factors is the same as at the time he was last in contact with the floor or an extension of the floor such as a bleacher. When the ball touches an official, it is the same as touching the floor at the official's location.

SECTION 16. The **mid-court** area of a team is that part of its front court between the division line and a parallel imaginary line approximately 3 feet outside that part of the free throw circle which is farthest from the end line.

SECTION 17. A **multiple throw** is a succession of free throws attempted by the same team.

SECTION 18. A **pass** is movement of the ball caused by a player, who throws, bats or rolls the ball to another player.

SECTION 19. A **penalty for a foul** is the charging of the offender with the foul and awarding one or more free throws, or awarding the ball to the opponents for a throw-in. The penalty for a **violation** is the awarding of the ball to the opponents for a throw-in or one or more points or a substitute free throw.

SECTION 20. A **pivot** takes place when a player who is holding the ball steps once or more than once in any direction with the same foot, the other foot, called the pivot foot, being kept at its point of contact with the floor.

SECTION 21. A **rule** is one of the groups of laws which govern the game. A game law (commonly called a rule) sometimes states or implies the ball is dead or a foul or violation is involved. If it does not, it is assumed the ball is alive and no foul or violation has occurred to affect the given situation. A single infraction is not complicated by a second infraction unless so stated or implied.

SECTION 22. **Running with the ball** (traveling) is moving a foot or the feet in any direction in excess of prescribed limits while holding the ball. The limits follow:

Item 1. A player who receives the ball while standing still may pivot, using either foot as the pivot foot.

Item 2. A player, who receives the ball while his feet are moving or who is dribbling, may stop as follows:

(a) If he catches the ball while **both feet** are off the floor and:

    (1) **He alights with both feet** touching the floor simultaneously, he may pivot using either foot as the pivot foot; or

    (2) **He alights with first one foot** touching the floor followed by the other, he may pivot using the first foot to touch the floor as the pivot foot; or

    (3) **He alights on one foot,** he may jump off that foot and alight with both feet simultaneously but he may not pivot before releasing the ball.

(b) If he catches the ball while only **one foot** is off the floor:

    (1) **He may step** with the foot which is off the floor and may then pivot using the other foot as the pivot foot; or

    (2) **He may jump** with the foot which is on the floor and alight with both feet simultaneously, but he may not pivot before releasing the ball.

Item 3. After a player has come to a stop, he may pass or throw for goal under the following conditions:

(a) In Items 1, 2a(1), 2a(2) and 2b(1), he may **lift either foot,** but if he lifts his pivot foot or jumps before he passes or throws for goal, the ball must leave his hand before the pivot foot again touches the floor; or if he has jumped before either foot touches the floor.

(b) In Items 2a(3) and 2b(2), he may **lift either foot or jump** before he passes or throws for goal. However, the ball must leave his hand before a foot which has left the floor retouches it.

Item 4. A player who receives the ball as in Item 1 or a player, who comes to a stop after he receives the ball while he is moving his feet, may start a dribble under the following conditions:

(a) In Items 1, 2a(1), 2a(2) and 2b(1), the ball must leave his hand **before the pivot foot leaves the floor.**

(b) In Items 2a(3) and 2b(2), the ball must leave his hand **before either foot leaves the floor.**

    Ques. (1)—Is it traveling, if a player falls to the floor while holding the ball? Ans.—No, unless he makes progress by sliding.

    Ques. (2)—A1 jumps to throw the ball. B1 prevents the throw by placing one or both hands firmly on the ball so that: (a) A1; or (b) A1 and B1 both return to the floor holding it. Ans.—Held ball. However, if A1 voluntarily drops the ball before he returns to the floor and he then touches the ball before it is touched by another player, A1 has committed a traveling violation.

SECTION 23. A **screen** is legal action by a player who, without causing contact, delays or prevents an opponent from reaching a desired position.

SECTION 24. A throw-in is a method of putting the ball in play from out of bounds in accordance with Rule 7. The throw-in begins when the ball is at the disposal of the player or team entitled to it and ends when the passed ball touches or is touched by an inbounds player other than the thrower-in.

Section 25. A try for field goal is an attempt by a player to score 2 points by throwing the ball into his basket. The try starts when the player begins the motion which habitually preceeds the release of the ball. The try ends when the ball is clearly in flight.

SECTION 26. A violation is a rule infraction of the type listed in Rule 9.

Rule 5 Scoring and Timing Regulations

SECTION 1. A goal is made when a live ball enters the basket from above and remains in or passes through.
Ques.—If the ball enters the basket from below, goes through and drops back into the basket, is a goal scored? Ans.—No, it is a violation.

SECTION 2. A goal from the field counts 2 points for the team into whose basket the ball is thrown. A goal from a free throw is credited to the thrower and counts 1 point for his team.
NOTE—A field goal in A's basket after being last touched by B is not credited to any player but is mentioned in a footnote and two points are added to A's total.
Ques.—A player throws a field goal in his opponents' basket. Who gets credit for the goal? Ans.—It is not credited to a player. It is added to the opponents' score and mentioned in a footnote.

SECTION 3. The winning team is the one which has accumulated the greater number of points when the game ends.

SECTION 4. The referee shall forfeit the game if a team refuses to play after being instructed to do so by either official. If the team to which the game is forfeited is ahead, the score at the time of forfeiture shall stand. If this team is not ahead the score shall be recorded as 2-0 in its favor.
Ques.—When the game is forfeited, are the points made by each player credited to him? Ans.—The league officers should decide. It is customary to include such points in the scoring records.

SECTION 5. Playing time shall be: (a) for teams of college age, two halves of 20 minutes each with an intermission of 15 minutes between halves; (b) for teams of high school age, four quarters of 8 minutes each with intermissions of one minute after the 1st and 3rd quarters and 10 minutes between halves; (c) for teams younger than in (b), four quarters of 6 minutes each with intermissions the same as for (b).

SECTION 6. Each period begins when the ball first becomes alive. It ends when time expires except that: (a) if the ball is in flight after a try for field goal, the period ends when the ball goes through the basket; or it is certain the ball will not go through the basket; or when the ball, after the try is in flight, touches the floor or any player; or when the ball becomes dead; or (b) if a held ball occurs so near the expiration of time that the clock is not stopped before time expires, the period ends with the held ball; or (c) if a foul occurs so near the expiration of time that the timer cannot get the clock stopped before time expires or if the foul occurs after time expires but while the ball is in flight on a try for field goal, the period ends when the free throw or throws and all related activity have been completed.

SECTION 7. If the score is tied at the end of the second half, play shall continue without change of baskets for one or more extra periods with a one-minute intermission before each extra period. The game ends if, at the end of any extra period, the score is not tied.

In games played in halves, the length of each extra period shall be 5 minutes. In games played in quarters, the length of each extra period shall be 3 minutes. As many such periods as are necessary to break the tie shall be played. Extra periods are an extension of the 2nd half.

Ques.—With the score tied, a foul is committed near the expiration of time in the second half. If the free throw is successful, should an extra period be played? Ans.—If the foul occurs before the ball becomes dead and the period is ended as outlined in 5-6, no extra period is played. But if the foul occurs after the period has clearly ended, the extra period is played.

SECTION 8. Time-out occurs and the game watch, if running, shall be stopped when an official:

Item 1. Signals: (a) a foul; (b) held ball; or (c) a violation.

Item 2. Stops play: (a) because of an injury; (b) to confer with scorers or timers; (c) because of unusual delay in getting a dead ball alive; or (d) for any emergency.

Item 3. Grants a player's request for a time-out, such request being granted only when the ball is dead or in control of a player of his team and when no change of status of the ball is about to occur.

Item 4. Responds to the scorer's signal to grant a coach's request that a correctable error be prevented or rectified. Such a request shall be presented while the ball is dead and the clock is stopped. The appeal to the official shall be presented at the scorer's table when a coach of each team may be present.

NOTE—When a player is injured as in Item 2(a), the official may suspend play when the ball is dead or is in control of the injured player's team or when the opponents complete a play. A play is completed when a team loses control (including throwing for goal), or withholds the ball from play by ceasing to attempt to score or advance the ball to a scoring position. When necessary to protect an injured player, the official may suspend play immediately.

SECTION 9. A time-out shall be charged to a team for each minute or fraction of a minute consumed under Items 2(a), 3 and 4 of Section 8.

EXCEPTIONS: No time-out is charged:

(a) If in Item 2(a) an injured player is ready to play immediately or is replaced within 1½ minutes; or

(b) If in Item 3 the player's request results from displaced eyeglasses or lens; or

(c) If in Item 4 a correctable error is prevented or rectified; or

(d) If a disqualified player is replaced within 1 minute.

SECTION 10. After time has been out, the game watch shall be started when the official signals time-in. If official neglects. to signal, the timer is authorized to start the watch unless an official specifically signals continued time-out.

    a. If play is resumed by a jump, the watch shall be started when the tossed ball is legally tapped.

    b. If a free throw is not successful and ball is to remain alive, the watch shall be started when the ball is touched or touches a player on the court.

    c. If play is resumed by a throw-in, the watch shall be started when the ball touches or is touched by a player on the court.

    Ques.—During a free throw which is not successful, a violation occurs. Should the clock be started when the ball is touched or touches a player on the court? **Ans.**—No and official should avoid using the time-in chopping motion, if the ball is not to remain alive.

SECTION 11. Five charged time-outs may be granted each team during an untied game. During each extra period, each team is always entitled to at least one time-out. Unused time-outs accumulate and may be used at any time. Time-outs in excess of the allotted number may be granted at the expense of a technical foul for each.

Rule 6   Live Ball and Dead Ball

SECTION 1. The game shall be started by a jump ball in the center circle. After any subsequent dead ball, play shall be resumed by a jump ball or by a throw-in or by placing it at the disposal of a free thrower. The ball becomes alive when: (a) on a jump ball, the ball leaves the official's hand; or (b) on a throw-in, the ball touches a player who is inbounds; or (c) on a free throw, the ball is placed at the disposal of the free thrower.

SECTION 2. The ball shall be put in play in the center circle by a jump between two opponents: (a) at the beginning of each quarter and extra period; or (b) after a double foul; or (c) after the last free throw following a false double foul.

    Ques.—Does a quarter, half or extra period start with a jump ball if a foul occurs before the ball becomes alive? **Ans.**—No. Any rules statement is made on the assumption that no infraction is involved unless mentioned or implied. If such infraction occurs, the rule governing it is followed in accordance with Rule 4-21.

SECTION 3. The ball shall be put in play by a jump ball at the center of the restraining circle which is nearest the spot where: (a) a held ball occurs; or (b) the ball goes out of bounds as in 7-3; or (c) a double free throw violation occurs; or (d) the ball lodges on a basket support; or (e) the ball becomes dead when neither team is in control and no goal or infraction or end of a period is involved. In (a) or (b), the jump shall be between the two involved players unless injury or disqualification requires substitution for a jumper, in which case his substitute shall jump. In (c), (d), and (e), the jump shall be between any two opponents.

SECTION 4. For any jump ball, each jumper shall have one or both feet on or inside that half of the jumping circle (imaginary if in a free throw restraining circle) which is farther from his own basket. An official shall then toss the ball upward between the jumpers in a plane at right angles to the sidelines, to a height greater than either of them can jump and so that it will drop between them. The ball must be tapped by one or both of the jumpers after it reaches its highest point. If it touches the floor without being tapped by at least one of the jumpers, the official shall toss the ball again.

Neither jumper shall: tap the tossed ball before it reaches its highest point; nor leave the jumping circle until the ball has been tapped; nor catch the jump ball; nor touch it more than twice. The jump ball and these restrictions end when the tapped ball touches one of the eight non-jumpers, the floor, the basket or the backboard.

None of the 8 non-jumpers shall have either foot in the restraining circle cylinder until the ball has been tapped. Teammates may not occupy adjacent positions around the restraining circle if an opponent indicates his desire for one of these positions before the official is ready to toss the ball.

Ques.—During jump ball, is a jumper required to: (a) face his own basket; and (b) jump and attempt to tap the tossed ball? Ans.—(a) No specific facing is required. However, a jumper must be in the proper half of the jumping circle. (b) No. But if neither jumper taps the ball, it should be tossed again with both jumpers being ordered to jump.

SECTION 5. The ball shall be put in play by a throw-in under circumstances as outlined in Rules 7, 8-5 and 9-1 to 11.

SECTION 6. The ball shall be put in play by placing it at the disposal of a free thrower before each free throw.

SECTION 7. The ball becomes dead or remains dead when:

    a. Any goal is made as in 5-1;

    b. It is apparent the free throw will not be successful: on a free throw for a technical foul or a false double foul, or a free throw which is to be followed by another throw;

    c. Held ball occurs or ball lodges on the basket support;

    d. Official's whistle is blown;

    e. Time expires for a quarter, half or extra period;

    f. A foul occurs: or

    g. Any floor violation (9-2 to 10) occurs, or there is basket interference (9-11), or there is a free throw violation by the thrower's team (9-1).

EXCEPTION: The ball does not become dead when: (1) d, e or f occurs after a try for a field goal is in flight; or (2) d or f occurs after a try for a free throw is in flight; or (3) a foul is committed by an opponent of a player who has started a try for goal before the foul occurred provided time did not expire before the ball was in flight. The trying motion must be continuous and begins after the ball comes to rest in the player's hand or hands and is completed when the ball is clearly in flight. The trying motion may include arm, foot, or body movements used by the player when throwing the ball at his basket.

Ques.—If the ball is in flight after A's try for field goal when time for the period expires, and if the ball is subsequently touched, does the goal count if made? Ans.—No. The try ends when ball is touched. If it is basket interference (9-11) by B, 2 points are awarded to A.

132

Rule 7 Out of Bounds and the Throw-In

SECTION 1. A player is out of bounds when he touches the floor or any object on or outside a boundary. For location of a player in the air, see 4-15.

The ball is out of bounds when it touches: a player who is out of bounds; or any other person, the floor, or any object on or outside a boundary; or the supports or back of the backboard; or ceiling, overhead equipment or supports.

NOTE—When the rectangular backboard is used, the ball is out of bounds if it passes over the backboard.

Ques. (1)—Ball rebounds from the edge of backboard and across boundary line, but before it touches the floor or any obstruction out of bounds, it is caught by a player who is inbounds. Is the ball inbounds or out of bounds? Ans.—Inbounds.

Ques. (2)—The ball touches or rolls along the edge of the backboard without touching the supports. Is the ball dead? Ans.—No, unless ground rules to the contrary have been mutually agreed upon before the game.

SECTION 2. The ball is caused to go out of bounds by the last player to touch it before it goes out, provided it is out of bounds because of touching something other than a player.

If the ball is out of bounds because of touching a player who is on or outside a boundary, such player causes it to go out.

Ques. (1)—Live ball is held by A. (a) The ball held by or passed by A touches B when B is on or outside the boundary; or (b) the ball is batted to out of bounds by B who is inbounds. Ans.—Ball awarded to A for a throw-in.

Ques. (2)—Ball passed by A touches an official and goes out of bounds. Whose ball? Ans.—B's ball.

SECTION 3. If the ball goes out of bounds and was last touched simultaneously by two opponents, both of whom are inbounds or out of bounds, or if the official is in doubt as to who last touched the ball, or if the officials disagree, play shall be resumed by a jump ball between the two involved players in the nearest restraining circle.

SECTION 4. The ball is awarded out of bounds after: (a) a violation as in Rule 9; or (b) a free throw for a technical foul as in Rule 8-5-b; or (c) a field goal or a successful free throw for personal foul as in 8-5-a or an awarded goal as in 9-11; or (d) the ball becomes dead while a team is in control provided no infraction or the end of a period is involved; or (e) a player control foul.

SECTION 5. a. When the ball is out of bounds after any violation as outlined in sections 2 through 11 in Rule 9, the official shall designate a nearby opponent of the player who committed the violation, and he shall hand the ball to this player or his substitute for a throw-in from the designated spot nearest the violation, except as indicated in the penalties which follow Rule 9-10 and 11.

b. After a dead ball, as listed in section 4 (d), any player of the team in control shall make the throw-in from the designated out of bounds spot nearest to the ball when it became dead.

c. After a player control foul, any player of the offended team shall make the throw-in from the designated spot nearest the foul, except that, if the ball has passed through the basket during the dead ball period immediately following the foul, no point can be scored and the ball is awarded to any player of the offended team out of bounds at either end of that free throw line extended which is nearer the goal through which the ball was thrown.

d. If in items a, b or c, the throw-in spot is behind a backboard, the throw-in shall be made from the nearer free throw lane line extended.

e. After a goal as listed in section 4 (c), the team not credited with the score shall make the throw-in from the end of the court where the goal was made and from any point outside the end line. Any player of the team may make a direct throw-in or he may pass the ball along the end line to a teammate behind the line.

f. After a technical foul, any player of the team to whom the free throw has been awarded shall make the throw-in from out of bounds at mid-court on either side.

g. After a free throw violation by the throwing team as listed in section 1 of rule 9, any opponent of the throwing team shall make the throw-in from out of bounds at either end of the free throw line extended.

SECTION 6. **The throw-in starts** when the ball is at the disposal of a player entitled to the throw-in and he shall pass the ball directly into the court so that, after it crosses the boundary line and before going out of bounds, it touches or is touched by another player on the court within 5 seconds from the time the throw-in starts. Until the passed ball has crossed the plane of the boundary: (a) the thrower shall not leave the designated throw-in spot; (b) no player shall have any part of his person over the boundary line; and (c) teammates shall not occupy adjacent positions near the boundary if an opponent desires one of the positions. The 3-foot restraining line is sometimes the temporary boundary as in rule 1-2.

Question.—B has the ball out of bounds. His throw-in: (a) enters a basket before touching anyone; or (b) strikes ring or backboard and rebounds; or (c) touches another player and then enters basket. Ans.—(a) Violation by B. A's ball at either end of the nearer free throw line extended. No goal because ball is dead. (b) Ball becomes alive when touched. (c)—Legal goal for team in whose basket the ball remains or through which it passes.

Rule 8   Free Throw

SECTION 1. **When a free throw is awarded,** an official shall take the ball to the free throw line of the offended team. After allowing reasonable time for players to take their positions, he shall put the ball in play by placing it at the disposal of the free thrower. The same procedure shall be followed for each free throw of a multiple throw. During a free throw for personal foul, each of the lane spaces adjacent to the end line shall be occupied by one opponent of the free thrower. A teammate of the free thrower is entitled to the next adjacent lane space on each side and to each other alternate position along each lane line. Not more than one player may occupy any part of the first, second or third lane spaces. If the ball is to become dead when the last free throw for a specific penalty is not successful, players shall not take positions along the free throw lane.

NOTE—To avoid disconcerting the free thrower, neither official should stand in the free throw lane or the lane extended.

SECTION 2. **The free throw or throws awarded** because of a personal foul shall be attempted by the offended player. If such player must withdraw because of an injury or disqualification, his substitute shall attempt the throw or throws unless no substitute is available, in which event any teammate may attempt the throw or throws.

SECTION 3. The free throw awarded because of a technical foul may be attempted by any player, including an entering substitute, of the offended team.

SECTION 4. The try for goal shall be made within 10 seconds after the ball has been placed at the disposal of the free thrower at the free throw line. This shall apply to each free throw.

SECTION 5. After a free throw which is not followed by another free throw, the ball shall be put in play by a throw-in: **(a)** as after a field goal (7-5) if the try is for a personal foul and is successful; or **(b)** by any player of the free thrower's team from out of bounds at mid-court if the free throw is for a technical foul.

SECTION 6. If a free throw for a personal foul is unsuccessful, or if there is a multiple throw for a personal foul (or fouls) and the last free throw is unsuccessful, the ball remains alive.

If there is a multiple throw and both a personal and technical foul are involved, the tries shall be attempted in the order in which the related fouls were called and if the last try is for a technical foul the ball shall be put in play as after any technical foul.

SECTION 7. After the last free throw following a false double foul (4-8(b)), the ball shall be put in play by a jump at center between any two opponents.

Ques.—Two free throws are awarded to A and before time is in, one free throw is awarded to B. What is the correct procedure? Ans.—Jump ball at center after the third free throw.

Rule 9 Violations and Penalties

A player shall not—

SECTION 1. Violate the free throw provisions: (a) The try shall be attempted from within the free throw circle and behind the free throw line. (b) After the ball is placed at the disposal of a free thrower: (1) he shall throw within 10 seconds and in such a way that the ball enters the basket or touches the ring before the free throw ends; (2) no opponent may disconcert the free thrower; and (3) the free thrower shall not have either foot beyond the vertical plane of that edge of the free throw line which is farther from the basket; and no other player of either team shall have either foot beyond the vertical plane or cylinder of the outside edge of any lane boundary, nor beyond the vertical plane of any edge of the space (2 inches by 36 inches) designated by a lane space mark or the space (12 inches by 36 inches) designated by a neutral zone mark, nor enter nor leave the lane space which is nearest the end line. The restrictions in (3) apply until the ball touches the ring or backboard or until the free throw ends. (c) An opponent of the free thrower shall occupy each lane space adjacent to the end line during the try, and no teammate of the free thrower may occupy either of these lane spaces.

PENALTY—(1) If violation is by the free thrower or his teammate only, no point can be scored by that throw. Ball becomes dead when violation occurs. Ball is awarded out of bounds on the sideline to the free thrower's team opposite center circle after a technical foul, and to any opponent out of bounds at either end of the free throw line extended after a personal foul. (2) If violation is by the free thrower's opponent only: if the try is successful, the goal counts and violation is disregarded; if it is not successful, a substitute throw shall be attempted by the same thrower under conditions the same as for the throw for which it is substituted. In these cases, ball becomes dead when the free throw ends. (3) If there is a violation by each team, ball becomes dead when violation by the free thrower's team occurs, no point can be scored, and play shall be resumed by a jump between any two opponents in the nearest circle. The out of bounds provision in penalty item (1) and the jump ball provision in penalty item (3) do not apply if the free throw is to be followed by another free throw, or if there are free throws by both teams. In penalty item (3), if an opponent of the thrower touches the free throw before it has touched the ring, the violation for failure to touch the ring is ignored.

Ques.—During a free throw by A1, B1 pushes A2 and also B1 or B2 is in the lane too soon. Ans.—If the free throw is not successful, award a substitute free throw and also penalize the foul.

SECTION 2. Cause the ball to go out of bounds.

Ques.—Dribbler in control steps on or outside a boundary, but does not touch the ball while he is out of bounds. Is this a violation? Ans.—Yes.

SECTION 3. Violate provisions governing the throw-in. The thrower-in shall not: (a) leave the designated throw-in spot; (b) fail to pass the ball directly into the court so that after it crosses the boundary line it touches or is touched by another player on the court before going out of bounds; (c) consume more than 5 seconds from the time the throw-in starts until it touches or is touched by a player on the court; (d) carry the ball onto the court; (e) touch it in the court before it has touched another player; nor (f) throw the ball so that it enters a basket before touching anyone.

No player shall: (g) have any part of his person over the boundary line before the ball has been passed across the line; nor (h) become the thrower-in after an official has designated another player.

Ques.—On throw-in, A steps on the line or reaches through its plane while holding the ball. Ans.—Violation. Allowance should be made if space is limited.

SECTION 4. Run with the ball, kick it, strike it with the fist or cause it to enter and pass through the basket from below.

NOTE—Kicking the ball is a violation only when it is a positive act; accidentally striking the ball with the foot or leg is not a violation.

Ques.—What is kicking the ball? Ans.—Kicking the ball is striking it intentionally with the knee or any part of the leg or foot below the knee. It is a fundamental of basketball that the ball must be played with the hands.

SECTION 5. Dribble a second time after his first dribble has ended, unless it is after he has lost control because of: (a) a try for field goal after the ball is in flight; or (b) a bat by an opponent; or (c) a pass or fumble which has then touched another player. He shall not make more than one air dribble during a dribble.

SECTION 6. Violate any provision of 6-4. If both teams simultaneously commit violations during the jump ball, or if the official makes a bad toss, the toss should be repeated.

SECTION 7. Remain for more than 3 seconds in that part of his free throw lane between the end line and the farther edge of the free throw line while the ball is in control of his team. Allowance shall be made for a player who, having been in the restricted area for less than 3 seconds, dribbles in to try for goal.

Ques.—Does the 3-second restriction apply: (a) to a player who has only one foot touching the lane boundary ; or (b) while the ball is dead or is in flight on a try? Ans.—(a) Yes, the line is part of the lane. (b) No, the team is not in control.

SECTION 8. Be (and his team shall not be) in continuous control of a ball which is in his back court for more than 10 consecutive seconds.

SECTION 9. Be the first to touch a ball which he or a teammate caused to go from front court to back court by being the last to touch the ball while it was in control of his team and before it went to the back court. EXCEPTION: This restriction does not apply if, after a jump ball in the center circle, the player who first secures control of the tapped ball is in his front court at the time he secures such control and he causes the ball to go to his back court not later than the first loss of player control by him and provided it is the first time the ball is in his back court following the jump ball.

Ques.—A receives pass in his front court and throws ball to his back court where ball: (a) is touched by a teammate: or (b) goes directly out of bounds ; or (c) lies or bounces with all players hesitating to touch it. Ans.—Violation when touched in (a). In (b) it is a violation for going out of bounds. In (c) ball is alive so that B may secure control. If A touches ball first, it is a violation. The ball continues to be in team control of A and if A does not touch it the 10-second count starts when the ball arrives in the back court.

SECTION 10. Excessively swing his arms or elbows, even though there is no contact with an opponent.

PENALTY—(Sections 2 to 10): Ball becomes dead or remains dead when violation occurs. Ball is awarded to a nearby opponent for a throw-in at the out of bounds spot nearest the violation. If the ball passes through a basket during the dead ball period immediately following a violation, no point can be scored and the ball is awarded to an opponent out of bounds at either end of that free throw line extended nearer the goal through which the ball was thrown.

SECTION 11. (a) Touch the ball or basket when the ball is on or within either basket; nor touch the ball when it: (b) is touching the cylinder having the ring as its lower base; or (c) is not touching the cylinder but is in downward flight during a try for field goal while the entire ball is above the basket ring level and before the ball has touched the ring or the try has ended. Exception: In (a) or (b), if a player near his own basket has his hand legally in contact with the ball, it is not a violation if his contact with the ball continues after it enters the cylinder, or if, in such action, he touches the basket.

PENALTY—If violation is at the opponent's basket, offended team is awarded one point if during a free throw and two points in any other case. The crediting of the score and subsequent procedure is the same as if the awarded score had resulted from the ball having gone through the basket, except that the official shall hand the ball to a player of the team entitled to the throw-in.

If violation is at a team's own basket, no points can be scored and the ball is awarded to the offended team at the out of bounds spot on the side at either end of the free throw line extended.

If there is a violation by both teams, play shall be resumed by a jump ball between any two opponents in the nearest circle.

Ques.—While the ball is in flight on a try for field goal by A, a teammate of A pushes an opponent. After this personal foul, the ball is on the ring when B bats it away. Which infraction should be penalized? Ans.—Both. Award 2 points to A. Then penalize for personal foul.

Rule 10   Fouls and Penalties

A. TECHNICAL FOUL . . .

A team shall not—
SECTION 1. Delay the game by preventing ball from being promptly made alive, or by allowing the game to develop into an actionless contest.
This includes the following and similar acts:
(a) When clock is not running—consuming a full minute through not being ready when it is time to start either half; or
(b) Failure to supply scorers with data as outlined in rule 3-2; or
(c) When behind in the score or while on defense with the score tied and after a warning by an official, failing to be reasonably active in attempts to secure the ball if on defense or to advance the ball beyond the mid-court area if on offense and there is no opposing action in the mid-court area.

SECTION 2. Be charged with an excess time-out (5-11).

SECTION 3. Have more than five squad members participating simultaneously.
A player shall not—

SECTION 4. (a) Participate after changing his number without reporting it to the scorers and an official;
(b) Participate after having been disqualified;
(c) Attempt to gain an advantage: by interfering with ball after a goal or by failing to immediately pass ball to nearer official if in control when a violation is called, or by repeated infractions of 9-3g and h;
(d) Wear an illegal number;
(e) Grasp the basket;
(f) Leave the court for an unauthorized reason; or
(g) Purposely delay his return to the court after being legally out of bounds.

Ques.—A player steps out of bounds to avoid contact. Ans.—This is not a foul unless he leaves to conceal himself or to deceive in some other way. If he is a dribbler, ball is out of bounds.

SECTION 5. Use unsportsmanlike tactics, such as: (a) disrespectfully addressing or contacting an official, or failing to raise his hand at arm's length above his head after being charged with a foul or raising it in such a way as to indicate resentment; (b) using profanity; (c) baiting an opponent or obstructing his vision by waving hands near his eyes; (d) climbing on a teammate to secure greater height to handle ball; (e) knowingly attempting a free throw to which he was not entitled; or (f) causing unsportsmanlike contact as in 4-8 (i).

NOTE—Contact after the ball has become dead is ignored unless it is unsportsmanlike or is during a throw-in.

A substitute shall not—
SECTION 6. Enter the court: (a) without reporting to scorers; or (b) without his name appearing on the pregame squad list; or (c) (unless between halves) without being beckoned by an official.

A coach, substitute, team attendant or follower shall not—
SECTION 7. Disrespectfully address an official nor attempt to influence his decisions; nor disrespectfully address or bait an opponent; nor indicate his objection to an official's decision by rising from the bench or using gestures; nor do anything to incite undesirable crowd reactions; nor shall he enter the court unless by permission of an official to attend an injured player. Coaches shall remain seated on the bench except, while the clock is stopped, they may leave the bench to direct or encourage players who are on the court. Coaches may, at any time, leave the bench to confer with substitutes, to signal players to request a time-out, or to perform other necessary coaching responsibilities. During an intermission or a time-out charged to a team, the coach and/or team attendants may confer with their players at or near their bench.

PENALTY—(Sections 1 to 7): Offended team is awarded one free throw and its captain shall designate the thrower. A second free throw shall be awarded if the foul is flagrant. EXCEPTION: If more than one infraction by the same team is involved in section 1(a) or 4(d), or if two or more teammates are involved in sections 3 or 6, only one free throw is awarded.

For sections 3 and 4 (a) or (b), an infraction shall be penalized if it is discovered during the time the rule is being violated or an error for failure to penalize may be corrected by applying rule 2-10.

For sections 4(a) and (b), or for flagrant or persistent infraction of any section, the offender shall be disqualified. If the offender is a coach, substitute, team attendant or follower, he shall be banished from the vicinity of the court. For failure to comply, referee may forfeit the game.

B. PERSONAL FOUL . . .

SECTION 8. A player shall not: hold, push, charge, trip; nor impede the progress of an opponent by extended arm, shoulder, hip or knee, or by bending the body into other than a normal position; nor use any rough tactics. He shall not contact an opponent with his hand unless such contact is only with the opponent's hand while it is on the ball and is incidental to an attempt to play the ball. Contact caused by a defensive player approaching the ball holder from behind is a form of pushing and that caused by the momentum of a player who has thrown for goal is a form of charging.

A dribbler shall not charge into nor contact an opponent in his path nor attempt to dribble between two opponents or between an opponent and a boundary, unless the space is such as to provide a reasonable chance for him to go through without contact. If a dribbler, without contact, passes an opponent sufficiently to have head and shoulders in advance of him, the greater responsibility for subsequent contact is on the opponent. If a dribbler in his progress has established a straight line path, he may not be crowded out of that path but, if an opponent is able legally to establish a defensive position in that path, the dribbler must avoid contact by changing direction or ending his dribble.

A player who screens shall not: (a) when he is behind a stationary opponent, take a position closer than a normal step from him; (b) when he assumes a position at the side or in front of a stationary opponent, make contact with him; (c) take a position so close to a moving opponent that this opponent cannot avoid contact by stopping or changing direction. In (c), the speed of the player to be screened will determine where the screener may take his stationary position. This position will vary and may be one to two normal steps or strides from his opponent. (d) Move after assuming his screening position, except in the same direction and path of his opponent.

If the screener violates any of these provisions and contact results, he has committed a personal foul.

PENALTY—Offender is charged with one foul and if it is his fifth personal foul, or if it is flagrant, he is disqualified. (1) Offended player (or his substitute, if such player is disqualified or injured) is awarded one free throw unless it is a double foul or a player control foul. (2) Unless it is a multiple foul, a second free throw is awarded if the foul: (a) is flagrant or intentional, including one by a player who does not make reasonable effort to avoid contact and who tries to reach the ball from an unfavorable position; or (b) is committed against a field goal thrower whose try is not successful; or (c) is a common foul (except as noted in (1) above) which occurs after the offending team has been charged during the half with four personal fouls in a game played in quarters or with six personal fouls in a game played in halves, and provided the first free throw for the common foul is successful. (Extra periods are an extension of the 2nd half.)

NOTE—If there is any doubt as to whether there is player control during the time he or a teammate commits a common foul, the interpretation shall be that the ball was in player control.

Ques. (1)—A guard moves into the path of a dribbler and contact occurs. Who is responsible? Ans.—Either may be responsible but the greater responsibility is that of the dribbler if the guard conforms to the following principles which officials use in reaching a decision. The guard is assumed to have established a guarding position if he is in the dribbler's path facing him. No specific stance or distance is specified. It is assumed the guard may shift to maintain his position in the path of the dribbler provided he does not charge into the dribbler nor otherwise cause contact as outlined in the 2nd paragraph of 10-8. However, if he jumps into position, both feet must return to the floor after the jump, before he has established guarding position.

The responsibility of the dribbler for contact is not shifted merely because the guard turns or ducks to absorb shock when contact caused by the dribbler is imminent. The guard may not cause contact by moving under or in front of a passer or thrower after he is in the air with feet off the floor.

Ques. (2)—One or both fouls of either a multiple foul or of a double foul is flagrant. What is the procedure? Ans.—For a multiple foul, one free throw is awarded for each foul. For a double foul no free throws are awarded. In either case, any player who commits a flagrant foul is disqualified.

Ques. (3)—Does goal count if ball goes in the basket after a foul? Ans.—Yes, unless ball becomes dead (as in rule 6-7) before it enters the basket.

Index